Audiences

Audiences

A Sociological Theory *of* Performance *and* Imagination

Nicholas Abercrombie & Brian Longhurst

SAGE Publications
London • Thousand Oaks • New Delhi

SAGE Publications Ltd
6 Bonhill Street
London EC2A 4PU

SAGE Publications Inc
2455 Teller Road
Thousand Oaks, California 91320

SAGE Publications India Pvt Ltd
32, M-Block Market
Greater Kailash-I
New Delhi 110 048

British Library Cataloguing in Publication data

A catalogue record for this book is available from the British Library

ISBN 0 8039 8961 X
ISBN 0 8039 8962 8 (pbk)

Library of Congress catalog card number 97-062467

Typeset by Photoprint, Torquay, Devon
Printed in Great Britain by The Cromwell Press Ltd, Trowbridge, Wiltshire

Contents

Acknowledgements

As always, a large number of people have participated in the writing of this book. NA would particularly like to thank Baz Kershaw, Maria Shevstova and Nigel Whiteley for their guidance in new territory. He would also like to pay tribute – again – to the extraordinary intellectual atmosphere of the University of Lancaster.

BL has found discussions of various audiences with Gaynor Bagnall, Tony Kearon, Tony King, Jason Rutter and Greg Smith of great help, particularly in the stimulation of ideas and the comparison of different contexts and approaches. Thanks as ever to Bernadette Oxley, James Oxley-Longhurst and Tim Oxley-Longhurst for performances, audience activity and much more.

For
Harry Patterson and to the memory of Betty Patterson
and for
Bernadette, James and Tim

Introduction

Audiences are problematic. From both left and right they have been the subject of concern and debate. On the one hand, this has been expressed through fears about the effects of the mass media on a variety of different audiences; on the other, there is worry about the role of the media in the ideological framing of responses to key issues. Given the centrality of these debates, which recur perennially within media discourse itself, it is not surprising that the study of audiences has represented a key growth area of activity in the social sciences and humanities in recent times. There is now a vast amount of research and many books and articles on the audience, in particular the audience for television. Our view is that many of the fears and conventional debates about the audience are seriously misplaced. In this book, therefore, we want to argue for a new way of understanding the development of audience research and more importantly for conceptualizing the current accumulation of evidence on audience processes. Our book thus characterizes the past, classifies the present, and points to the future.

To develop our argument we have organized the book into six chapters. We begin by arguing that research into audiences has been structured by three paradigms. The development and main concerns of the first two of these paradigms are outlined in Chapter 1, which also suggests that these paradigms are, and should be, superseded by a third. The characterization of this paradigm and arguments for its power to understand contemporary audiences are set out in the rest of the book. We argue that to understand this paradigm, and audiences, it is important first to distinguish three different types of audience: simple, mass and diffused. This we do in Chapter 2. We shall argue that the diffused audience and the interactions between the three audience types can only be understood through the lens of the paradigm we shall label as Spectacle/Performance.

The most important general dimensions of the Spectacle/ Performance paradigm are outlined in Chapters 3 and 4. Chapter 3 identifies and characterizes what we shall call a circuit of spectacle and narcissism. Here we point to the centrality of performance, the way in which spectacle leads to the aestheticization of everyday life, and the constitution of the narcissistic society of modernity. Chapter 4 develops this argument through the consideration of the resources which drive and fuel the circuit. Here we emphasize the role of imagination and fantasy in the construction of community.

Chapter 5 develops these themes in a more specific way. Taking up contemporary arguments about fans and enthusiasts, it points to the power of the Spectacle/Performance paradigm in understanding the complexity of the interactions in the contemporary audience and identifies a continuum in the audience, which is characterized as differentially skilful and productive. Further, Chapter 6 locates our argument in terms of other issues in current sociological concern. We shall suggest that consideration of audience issues leads, *inter alia*, to new understandings of phenomena of trust and social inclusion and exclusion. Thus, in ways that we hope will become clear, and perhaps controversial, we see this as not simply another book about audiences (and more particularly the television audience), but an argument that modern advanced capitalist societies, and the processes of sociation characteristic of them, cannot be understood adequately without seeing them as characterized by relationships between performances and audiences in the senses we shall identify.

1

Changing Audiences; Changing Paradigms of Research

It is the purpose of this chapter to suggest that audiences for television, music, books, magazines, and so on, are changing together with wider social and cultural changes in society. In reviewing the argument and evidence for these changes, it is unfortunately often difficult to disentangle the real changes in the cultural forms, and the ways in which they are appropriated, from the changing frameworks within which researchers talk about those changes. In other words, what appear to be changes in the real world of the media *may* instead reflect, partly or wholly, changes in the ideas or concepts that inform and regulate the study of the media. Such a distinction is often captured by the use of the term 'paradigm'. However, our use of the concept differs somewhat from that classically proposed by Kuhn (1970) in that we wish to claim that successive paradigms give a better account of the world in certain respects. Hence, by paradigm we mean: a network of assumptions which prescribe what kinds of issues are proper research problems. Other issues which fall outside the paradigm are simply not researchable. Some problems are given a high priority while others are demoted. To a certain extent, the construction of a paradigm boundary, and the prioritizing of research problems, are the products of the interests of the community of researchers which may be independent of actual changes in the world. Within the paradigm, what goes on most of the time is the ordinary solving of problems, Kuhn's 'normal science'. B eventually, problems arise which cannot be solved within the paradigm boundary and the paradigm breaks up to be replaced by another one. These 'destructive' problems may be partly generated by the paradigm itself but will also arise out of changes in the world. In this sense, a paradigm may be a better account of the world than a preceding one to the extent that it addresses itself to the changes.

In what follows, we want to argue that audience research has, in the past fifty years or so, moved through three paradigms, Behavioural (BP), Incorporation/Resistance (IRP) and Spectacle/Performance (SPP). The identification of these three paradigms will emerge through a short history of audience research.

THE PHASES OF AUDIENCE RESEARCH

Typically, histories of audience research in the media divide up that history into phases, or periods. As far as television and radio are concerned, a common analysis is of three phases – 'effects', 'uses and gratifications' and 'encoding/decoding'.

Research on the effects of the media has been characterized by concerns about the potentially pernicious effects of the mass media of communication. These concerns and fears can be grouped into the following clusters: sexual activity; violence; children; elections and politics; gender; and race. Some social groups, and within these groups particular individuals, are held to be potentially especially susceptible to media messages. Thus, for example, children are often written about and considered to be particularly influenced by television in general and by representations of sex and violence more specifically. Moreover, the media are often thought to have long-run and general effects on patterns of gender and racial inequality through the selection and emphasis of a narrow range of images and representations of women and black people.

The earliest attempts at investigation of these effects of the mass media were undertaken from within the mass society or mass culture approach, which was given a particular impetus in this ﬁeld by the rise of, and use of mass media of communication by, fascist and totalitarian governments in the 1920s and 1930s. In simple terms the rise of industrialism or industrial capitalism had been seen to have broken the previous traditional links between people and social groups, leading to the generation of a mass of individuals who lacked true individuality and, in some accounts, discrimination.

In the more right-wing versions of this theory, the masses were feared in that they would tend to invade and hence corrupt the good government undertaken by more learned and aristocratic elite groups. Democracy was then a problem. In more left-wing variants, the fear or concern was that the mass of individuals would be easily open to the manipulation of the elite. This manipulation would take place though media like newspapers, radio and cinema, where alternative sources of information were either censored or had atrophied due to the break up of tradition and social networks.

In the earliest versions of effects research the effects of the media on the bare individuals of mass society were held to be fairly direct and unmediated. As many commentators have stated, the essential model here is of the media as a narcotic where messages are injected into the mass audience as if from a hypodermic syringe. The audience in turn responds to this stimulus in a fairly direct manner. As McQuail (1994, p. 338) suggests, in its simplest version, the notion of effect presupposes that the individual receiver of a single media message reacts to it directly.

The problems of this sort of effects model are well known. Contemporary media audiences do not simply consist of a mass of separated individuals; rather they are made up of complex and interacting social groups and individuals. Furthermore, the audience does not simply respond to the media message; it interacts with it in a variety of different ways. In addition, the messages contained in the mass media are not always simple and straightforward; rather they are complex and reasonably diverse. Finally, individuals in the real social world do not simply respond to messages, as if to an injection or stimulus. Such a naive behaviourist model of the individual cannot be sustained. However, in public debate the approach is still quite influential. For example

Walser (1993) shows how attempts to censor rock lyrics in the USA have been based on a direct-effect model of how audiences respond to music. Certain individuals are held to be susceptible to the messages which can cause them to behave in certain deviant ways, including suicide. As the relevant court cases have shown, these effects cannot be identified with any degree of legal certainty (see Longhurst, 1995, pp. 196–8; Walser, 1993).

As media effects research has developed it has become increasingly sophisticated, moving away from the simplicities of its earlier formulations and the stereotype of the injection model. However, it still shares some recognizable features with its beginnings, which demonstrate continuities in approach. Thus, McLeod et al. (1991) argue that the effects approach focuses on the ways in which audiences are affected or influenced by the media. It investigates such effects of influences empirically using quantitative methods based on the correlation of variables. Moreover, this approach has developed a number of different dimensions for the conceptualization of effects. Thus effects can be considered at the micro or macro level. They can be discussed in terms of the alteration of views and behaviour or of the stabilization and reinforcement of previously existing views and behaviour. In addition they can be seen as cumulative or non-cumulative and as short- or long-term. Furthermore, effects are hypothesized to occur in attitudes, cognition or behaviour. They can be seen as diffuse and general or viewed in content-specific terms. However, despite its continuing increased terminological, conceptual and methodological sophistication, the effects approach can be seen to have had at best inconclusive results. Nevertheless, perhaps the most significant form of contemporary effects research, cultivation analysis, has been argued to have demonstrated recognizable cultivation effects of mass media.

The cultivation approach, which was initiated by Gerbner in the 1960s, examines the 'relationships between exposure to television messages and audience beliefs and behaviours' (Morgan and Signorelli, 1990, p. 15). The focus of the approach is on the long-term effects of 'cumulative exposure' to media. More specifically, he approach tries to ascertain if those who spend more time watching television are more likely to perceive the real world in ways that reflect the most common and repetitive messages and lessons of the television world, compared with people who watch less television but are otherwise comparable in important demographic characteristics. (Morgan and Signorelli, 1990, p. 16)

Cultivation analysis combines content analysis of media messages with survey methods for the study of the audience.

The adherents of the ongoing and developing research programme in cultivation analysis maintain that they have detected small cultivation effects, but perhaps the most significant finding is what they have called 'mainstreaming', which means 'that heavy viewing may absorb or override differences in perspectives and behaviour that ordinarily stem from other factors and influences' (Morgan and Signorelli, 1990, p. 22). In conclusion, it is suggested that 'cultivation analysis has revealed that, in certain countries (notably the US), the more TV you watch, the more likely you are to have a fearful or distrustful attitude to the world outside' (Lewis, 1991, p. 19).

The effects research tradition, as the label suggests, has tended to focus upon the possible effects of the media upon the audience. The uses and gratifications approach takes the opposite stance, considering the uses made by the audience of media messages. The approach, which has its origins in studies carried out in the USA in the 1940s, emphasizes '(1) the social and psychological origins of (2) *needs*, which generate (3) expectations of (4) the mass media or other sources, which lead to (5) differential patterns of media exposure (or engagement in other activities), resulting in (6) need *gratifications* and (7) other consequences, perhaps mostly unintended ones' (Katz et al., 1974, p. 20).

Katz et al. argue that there are five elements to the uses and gratifications approach. First, the audience is seen as active; in particular it is 'goal-directed'. Second, audience members are seen to use their own initiative in linking the gratification of needs and choice. The individual uses the media, rather than being affected by it. Third, other sources can gratify these general and specific needs and 'media compete with other sources of need satisfaction'. Fourth, the uses and gratifications approach relies, in the main, on the self-reporting of motives for gratification by the audience member. Finally, the approach attempts to suspend value judgements about the media and the uses to which it is put.

Katz et al. further suggest that there were a number of developing issues and areas in the gratifications approach. First, they maintain that there was ongoing development in typologies of audience gratifications, in particular of the functions served by the media. They pointed, for example, to the functions of diversion, personal relations such as companionship, personal identity and surveillance (McQuail et al., 1972). Second, they suggested that further conceptualization of needs was required. Third, sources of media gratifications needed further explication; in particular consideration was needed of the relationship of media compared to other routes. Fourth, the relationship between gratifications and specific media attributes required further research, as did, fifth, whether these attributes were inherent in a particular medium such as film or radio. Sixth, there needed to be further consideration of the 'social origins of audience needs and their gratification', and, seventh, of the 'versatility of sources of need satisfaction', in that any one television programme or film could be hypothesized to satisfy a number of different needs. Finally, there needed to be consideration of the possibility of an integration or reconciliation of gratifications and effects research.

Like the effects approach, uses and gratifications has continued to develop along the lines set out by its initiators. Indeed, the approach has in certain respects benefited from the explosion of qualitative audience research which has occurred in the 1980s and 1990s, leading some commentators (see Ang, 1989) to suggest that there is a convergence between uses and gratifications and the more 'critical' approaches we discuss below. However, the approach has been subject to detailed criticism. One particular paper raises a number of points which have been significant in the development of audience studies.

Elliott (1974) argues that many of the problems of uses and gratifications stem from its emphasis on *needs* and *functions* and the assumptions upon which these concepts rest. More specifically, he argues that uses and gratifications is first of all 'mentalistic', in that it emphasizes the mental states of individuals. However, in Elliott's view, it is difficult to understand how these mental states can be known by the researcher at anything other than a superficial level. Second, the focus of the approach is essentially individualistic, in that it concerns itself with the individual and intra-individual processes. In these senses the approach is insufficiently sociological in Elliott's view. Furthermore, for Elliott, the approach is empiricist in that it lacks a prior social theory to guide research. Fourth, uses and gratifications engages in a form of static abstraction which isolates it claims for 'social process'. Consequently, the uses and gratifications approach is held to possess low explanatory power and to be inherently limited by its functionalism, with the familiar entailed traits of circularity, conservatism and insufficient attention to dysfunction.

It is not necessary to endorse Elliott's critique, which at the very least seems to bear the clear marks of the influence of certain forms of Marxism, to recognize that in many respects it points toward an alternative framework for the study of the media and audiences. This drive was realized in the encoding and decoding approach developed by Hall.

However, before pointing to the main features of this alternative approach it is worth recognizing the extent of ground shared by the effects and the uses and gratifications approaches. Three particular elements are important. First, the audience tends to be characterized on an essentially individualistic or society-wide level and there is a relative neglect of concrete social groups and their interactions. Thus, individuals are affected by media or use them, or society is led in particular directions. Second, the audience is affected by, or uses and responds to, a stimulus and there is a relative neglect of the analysis of texts and meanings, with the associated emphasis on the complexity of meaning and textual structure. Third, there is an emphasis on the functions of the media, in terms of propaganda and influence in campaigns for effects, or for the individual in terms of the satisfaction of needs for uses and gratifications. As we shall see below, these similarities have been pointed to by Hall in his attribution of the label of 'behaviourist' to these formulations.

In a very influential essay Hall (1982) provided a similar kind of history of audience research but self-consciously used the term 'paradigm' in much the same sense as we indicated above. Hall identifies a major paradigm shift in media studies, occurring in the 1970s, from a behavioural to a critical approach. The tradition of research in effects, cultivation, and uses and gratifications gave way to a different emphasis.

The first paradigm was behavioural in two main respects. First, the central question dominating research was whether the media had effects on the audience. 'These effects – it was assumed – could best be identified and analysed in terms of the changes which the media were said to have effected in the behaviour of individuals exposed to their influence' (p. 56). Second, the approach invoked a particular set of methodologies. Any claims about effects had to be subject to the sort of empirical test favoured by positivist social science. In Hall's view, these two features necessarily limited the scope of the approach. As he says:

> The model of power and influence being employed here was para-digmatically empiricist and pluralistic: its primary focus was the individual; it theorized power in terms of the direct influence of A on B's behaviour; it was preoccupied . . . with the process of decision-making. Its ideal experimental test was a before/after one: its ideal model of influence was that of the campaign. (p. 59)

The result was that a whole range of questions were necessarily unexamined:

> Larger historical shifts, questions of political process and formation before and beyond the ballot box, issues of social and political power, of social structure and economic relations, were simply absent, not by chance, but because they were *theoretically outside the frame of reference.* (p. 59)

Behind the limiting assumptions of the behavioural paradigm lay a particular model of society. Economic processes, class struc-tures and power relations were effectively ignored. Instead the model of society was an essentially cultural one in which societies are not riven by lines of structural conflict but are relatively harmonious and based on a shared consensus of values. The media were held to be expressive of this consensus. Their influence on the audience was largely one of reinforcement of the commonly held values of audience members.

On Hall's account the behavioural paradigm started to come apart because it was unable to solve a number of internal theoretical problems. Two of these were particularly important. First, the notion of a value consensus became difficult to sustain. Initially, those who did not share in this consensus were defined by the paradigm as deviants who were without any substantial system of values at all and were therefore peculiarly subject to media manipulation. Gradually it became clear that the differences between deviant or subcultural groups and the dominant culture were not natural but were rather socially constructed. There was no naturally defined value consensus on which everyone agreed but instead a socially enforced set of dominant values. 'In short, matters of cultural and social power – the power to define the rules of the game to which everyone was required to subscribe – were involved in the transactions between those who were consensus-subscribers and those who were labelled deviant' (p. 63). This alternative way of seeing the construction of a society's values has implications for the study of the media. No longer can the media be seen as the *expression* of a naturally occurring consensus. Instead they represent part of an effort to *impose* a set of values on a society.

The second way in which the behavioural paradigm faltered was closely related to the first. If the media were involved in constructing consent, they could no longer be seen as *reflecting* reality.

> But this threw into doubt the reflexive role of the media – simply showing things as they were – and it put into question the transparent conception of language which underpinned their assumed naturalism. For reality could no longer be viewed simply as a given set of facts: it was the result of a particular way of constructing reality. The media defined, not merely reproduced, 'reality'. (p. 64)

But if the media are *representing* reality rather than *reflecting* it, then they have to be seen as the creators of *meaning*, as 'signifying practices'. Furthermore, this will be a *particular* meaning.

These two breaches in the behavioural paradigm raise, for Hall, a whole series of questions that cannot be answered within the paradigm itself. The questions are, furthermore, all ones that are traditionally dealt with by the concept of ideology. A new paradigm is therefore necessary based on reformulations of the concept of ideology. This critical paradigm involves answers to two main questions. First, how does the ideological process work and what are its mechanisms? Second, how is the 'ideological' to be conceived in relation to other elements of the social structure?

The most important ideological mechanism lies in what is often called 'the circle of ideology'. Essentially, the proposition is that the media operate within a set of assumptions which are rarely articulated but which are nevertheless taken for granted. In operating in this way, the media effectively confirm the truth of the assumptions. The world is defined in terms of those assumptions and it is very difficult to think outside them because they structure the debate represented in the media. The media reinforce a dominant framework of values simply because they assume it and it becomes part of the audience's everyday world. For example, the Glasgow University Media Group (1980) argue that, in the debate about inflation in the 1970s, it was more or less assumed that inflation was caused by excessive wage demands. Debate in the media then took the form of argument as to whether wage demands were excessive and who was ultimately responsible for settling them. The debate was ideological in the sense that causes other than wage inflation were ruled out. The media operate within an unstated commonsense which is thereby confirmed. As Hall says: 'A similar case is the way in which the "problem of the welfare state" has come, in an era of economic recession and extreme monetarism, to be defined as the "problem of the scrounger", rather than the "problem of the vast numbers who could legally claim benefits, and need them, but don't"' (p. 81). To some extent the action of ideology here is a question of classification or framing. The events, personalities or ideas raised in the media do not come innocently at the audience; they are already classified by the background assumptions. Similarly, this notion of the media as ideological implies that ideology is not so much a *content* as a body of rules which generate the surface statements that appear in the media.

However, as Hall makes clear, one should be careful not to regard ideology as a fixed category. The output of the media is actually polysemic – potentially capable of several interpretations – even if one is preferred in the way that we have described. There is a *struggle* over meaning; different social groups aim to give their own meaning to events or ideas that receive public discussion. This struggle takes place in all sorts of different ways. At one level, for example, it involves a contest over the meaning or use of particular words. Hall points to the struggle to replace the term 'immigrant' with the term 'black'. 'But often, the struggle took the form of a different accenting of the same term: e.g. the process by means of which the derogatory colour "black" became the enhanced value "Black" (as in "Black is Beautiful")' (p. 78).

The answer to the second question concerning the relationship of ideological formations to the wider social structure is implied in the discussion of the first. In Hall's view there can be no recourse to a simple Marxism in which ideology can be read off from the economic structure. On the other hand, entirely to break the connexion between the ruling class and dominant ideas is to risk throwing the baby out with the bath-water. Hall's solution lies in the notion of hegemony.

Hegemony implied that the dominance of certain formations was secured, not by ideological compulsion, but by cultural leadership. It circumscribed all those processes by means of which a dominant class alliance or ruling bloc, which has effectively secured mastery over the primary economic processes in society, extends and expands its mastery over society in such a way that it can transform and re-fashion its way of life, its mores and conceptualization, its very form and level of culture and civilization in a direction which, while not directly paying immediate profits to the narrow interests of any particular class, favours the development and expansion of the dominant social and productive system of life as a whole. (p. 85)

As far as the media institutions are concerned, this means that they are both 'free of direct compulsion and constraint, and yet freely articulated themselves systematically around definitions of

the situation which favoured the hegemony of the powerful'
(p. 86). And

> To be impartial and independent in their daily operations, they cannot
> be seen to take directives from the powerful, or consciously to be
> bending their accounts of the world to square with dominant defini-
> tions. But they must be sensitive to, and can only survive legitimately
> by operating within, the general boundaries or framework of 'what
> everyone agrees' to: the consensus. (p. 87)

Hall (1980) had previously formulated similar arguments which
set out the parameters for what has become known as the encoding and decoding approach. As we have seen, two developments
were of particular importance. First, Hall argued that the study of
media communication had to be located within a Marxist understanding of the generation and distribution of power. Second, he
maintained that messages had to be understood through the
prism of semiotics. They were codes. Thus, media messages were
encoded from within the dominant frame or dominant global
ideology, by media personnel who operated professionally from
within the hegemonic order, often reproducing messages associated with political and economic elites. The messages contain
dominant or 'preferred meanings'.

These encoded messages were then decoded by audiences. An
important point here is that Hall breaks with simplistic Marxist
accounts which tend to assume that audiences can *only* work
within the false consciousness of the dominant frame. Rather, he
opens up the possibility that these are three positions from which
to decode media messages in general and television current affairs
texts in particular. Hall (1980) sees that there is transformation
taking place in research on the media and that 'there seems some
ground for thinking that a new and exciting phase in so-called
audience research, of a quite new kind may be opening up'
(p. 131).

Our argument in this chapter – and the rest of the book – is that
Hall's critical paradigm is itself being superseded. In order to see
how and why this is happening we need to look in more detail at
how the critical paradigm has developed over the last thirty years
or so. We argue that there have been subtle shifts in the manner in

which it has been deployed in both empirical and theoretical work. The emphasis on the role of the media as a site of *struggle* between incorporation and resistance has sharpened and, to signify this emphasis, we will re-christen the paradigm the Incorporation/Resistance paradigm.

THE INCORPORATION/RESISTANCE PARADIGM

The Incorporation/Resistance paradigm (IRP henceforth) defines the *problem* of audience research as whether audience members are incorporated into the dominant ideology by their participation in media activity or whether, to the contrary, they are resistant to that incorporation. It is very important to stress that the paradigm is defined by the *debate* between these two positions and not necessarily by the *endorsement* of one of them. Normal science is then the accumulation of evidence and argument around this debate. These are the questions that are permitted by the paradigm; other sorts of questions about the audience are almost un-askable or, at least, are not treated as serious or interesting contributions. Of course, not *all* studies in the media ask questions solely about incorporation or resistance; our claim is only that most do to the extent that these questions provide the dominant framework of analysis and empirical work.

In many ways, the paradigmatic empirical study within the IRP is Morley's (1980) investigation of television audiences for a current affairs programme, *Nationwide*, which, although somewhat elderly, is worth discussing in some detail. The study is partly a response to some features of the Behavioural paradigm, which, for Morley, is too individualistic and tends to emphasize individual psychologically based differences of interpretation.

> What is needed is an approach which links differential interpretations back to the socio-economic structure of society – showing how members of different groups and classes, sharing different cultural codes, will interpret a given message differently, not just at the personal/ idiosyncratic level, but in a way systematically related to their socio-economic position. (p. 88)

Morley argues that a useful way of doing this is to adapt Parkin's
(1971) theory of the way that members of different social classes
take up different views of the morality of social inequality. Using
this he proposes, following the paper on encoding and decoding
by Hall (1980) discussed earlier, that there are three positions that
an audience member may take towards an encoded message.

> He or she may take the meaning fully within the interpretative
> framework which the message itself proposes and prefers; if so,
> decoding proceeds within, or is aligned with, the dominant code.
> Second, the decoder may take the meaning broadly as encoded, but by
> relating the message to some concrete or situated context which
> reflects his/her position and interests, the reader may modify or
> partially inflect the given preferred meaning. Following Parkin, we
> can call this a 'negotiated' decoding. Third, the decoder may recognize
> how the message has been contextually encoded, but may bring to
> bear an alternative frame of reference which sets to one side the
> encoded framework and superimposes on the message an inter-
> pretation which works in a directly 'oppositional' way. (Morley, 1980,
> p. 89)

Although these three categories may be the most important,
Morley assumed that there would also be differences *within* them,
and his research design aimed to tap those internal differences in
interpretation.

Accordingly, Morley showed two *Nationwide* programmes –
which dealt with politically controversial topics – to twenty-nine
groups of people and tape-recorded a discussion that followed; he
then classified the responses manifested in those discussions in
terms of the dominant, negotiated or oppositional frameworks.
Each of the groups was composed of people representing a
particular socio-economic position. There were four main types –
managers, students, apprentices and trade-unionists – chosen on
the assumption that they would between them demonstrate the
three different kinds of responses. In turn, these four types were
subdivided. For trade-unionists, for example, there were groups
composed of trade-union officials and groups made up of shop
stewards. The manager category was made up of groups representing bank managers and print management trainees. To some
extent, the responses made by the groups accorded with the

hypothesis. Managers, for example, generally manifested a dominant coding. But the differences within the groups were also
important. Thus, shop stewards adopted a radical oppositional
response while trade-union officials demonstrated a negotiated
position. Within the student grouping the differences were even
more pronounced with black further education students adopting
oppositional positions, university arts students a negotiated one,
and apprentices a dominant one. Furthermore, the differences
within categories were not all along one dimension. So, although
shop stewards and black students are all resistant, they are not
resistant in the same way. The black students essentially with-
drew, considering the programme to be irrelevant to their concerns. The shop stewards, on the other hand, tended to be actively
critical, seeing *Nationwide* from a radical working-class perspective. Similarly, amongst those adopting the dominant mode there
are great differences. Bank managers were traditionally conserva-
tive. Apprentices, on the other hand, tended to be much more
cynical about people appearing on the programme, whoever they
were, but at the same time held 'dominant' attitudes on the evils
of trade-unionism or of the social security system.

Morley's path-breaking study tries to show how complex
responses to the media can be. In this sense it can be seen as a
reply to cruder versions of the IRP which insisted that responses
would be very simple, with respondents from subordinate classes
being ideologically incorporated within the dominant ideology
(see Abercrombie, et al., 1980, for an account). As Morley argues,
this complexity does not derive from individual idiosyncratic
difference. It is a function of socio-economic position but a complex one produced by the intersection of a variety of social,
cultural and discursive positions including class, ethnicity, age
and gender. But the important point to note is that, however
complex the positions may be, the crucial issue for Morley is the
relationship of those positions to the distribution of *power* and to a
particular account of that relationship, in which consent is secured
by the establishment of hegemony. 'Specifically, the project
attempted to relate the analysis of practices of "decoding" of
media material to the theoretical problematic centring on the
concept of hegemony' (Morley, 1980, p. 91). Such a focus clearly

limits the range of questions that can be asked of an audience's interpretations of media output of all kinds. That limitation is clearly indicated in Morley's use of Parkin's work as the starting point of a typology of audience decodings. Parkin's account is intended to provide a 'social perspective on the process of mass communication' which will 'divide and categorize the myriad individual variations in audience responses to media messages' (p. 88). But Parkin's is a *particular* kind of way of giving a social perspective which emphasizes the relationship to dominant ideology; there are, equally, many other dimensions of social life which will organize audience response, and consideration of these dimensions is effectively ruled out by the paradigm.

One can imagine extreme versions of working within the IRP. On the one hand, it could be argued that there is a uniform dominant ideology provided by the media which is uncritically taken up by audiences. The text is seen as monolithic, containing a well-marked preferred meaning making it difficult for alternative meanings to emerge. The audience is passive, the prisoner of the text, and is bound, therefore, to be very heavily influenced by the preferred meaning. This might be called the Dominant Text position. The contrary view of the relationship between text and audience might be called the Dominant Audience position. This tends to see the text not as monolithic with a strong preferred meaning, but rather as polysemic, containing a number of possible meanings and therefore allowing a range of audience interpretations. In turn, the audience is not passive in front of this more loosely organized text, but is active, discussing, analysing, ignoring, or rejecting the text. Such activity is more likely to lead to oppositional readings, to use Morley's terminology, although it may also allow neutral or playful readings.

These two positions occupy the extreme ends of a continuum and most work within the IRP operates within a narrower compass. So, there is some variation from those who find a preferred reading and a constrained audience to those who find polysemic texts and a resistant audience. A middling position is taken by those who find an audience active in making its own meanings but only within the constraints offered by the texts they appropriate. Some examples may help to make the variety of positions clearer.

An important variant of the Dominant Text view can be found in the mass culture critique produced by members of the Frankfurt School. Thus, for example, according to Adorno (1990), the listener to industrialized and commodified popular music is caught up in a standardized and routinized set of responses. In particular, Adorno argues that he or she is distracted and inattentive. In this sense, pop music is a part of the everyday background of contemporary social life. For example, we do not listen to it in the way that musical experts think that we should listen to a Beethoven symphony, that is, by sitting down and giving it all our attention, and seeing how the parts relate to the whole in creating the kind of meaning that Beethoven intended to communicate.

In Adorno's view, the pleasure derived from popular music is superficial and false. Thus the listener may be what Adorno calls 'rhythmically obedient'. He or she is a 'slave to the rhythm', following the standardized beat of the song and becoming over-powered by it. For Adorno, individuals who enjoy these pleasures are corrupted by immersion and are open to the domination of the industrialized, capitalist system. Another type of pleasure, which Adorno calls 'emotional', is also dangerous in his view. Feelings of emotion brought on by the popular song are false or immature, rather than deep or penetrating. For Adorno, there is no comparison between such feelings and the sorts of emotion which can be generated and expressed by the best forms of serious music.

It is important to note that Adorno recognized that even 'serious' music could be appropriated in such ways when it was transmitted through a mass medium. Standardized and emotional responses were not inherent in texts themselves but were produced by their dissemination by mass forms, such as radio. In Adorno's words:

In analyzing the fan mail of an educational station in a rural section of the Midwest, which has been emphasizing serious music at regular hours with a highly skilled and resourceful announcer, one is struck by the apparent enthusiasm of the listeners' reception, by the vast response, and by the belief in the highly progressive social function that this program is fulfilling. I have read all of these letters and cards very carefully. They are exuberant indeed. But they are enthusiastic in a manner that makes one feel uncomfortable. It is what might be called standardized enthusiasm. The communications are almost literally identical. (Adorno, 1993, p. 276)

A study by Philo (1990) illustrates a position further along the continuum. Philo investigated the responses of groups of television viewers to the British coal miners' strike of 1984–5. His method was to get his respondents to devise their own news programme about the strike, using a set of photographs supplied by Philo of various events during it. The study took place one year after the strike and, in consequence, its aim was not only to investigate what responses viewers had to the television presentation of the strike, but also to see what had stayed in their minds from the original broadcasts. From the evidence of the news programmes devised by his respondents and from the discussions involved in the making of the programmes, Philo concludes that there is considerable diversity in response. For example, there was very widespread agreement on the part of Philo's interviewees that television news at the time presented the strike in terms of the violence on the picket line. Violence constituted the agenda of television news. However, a substantial proportion of the viewers opposed this agenda, largely because they did not think that violence was the issue and the strike was not, in fact, particularly violent. A substantial proportion also believed that, to the extent that the strike was violent, this was not the fault of the miners, but was rather caused by the police or outside agitators. Viewers also differed by how much direct contact they had had with the events surrounding the strike. Those who had had such contacts were more likely to reject the agenda set by the television news, and such a tendency was unrelated to the social background of the viewers. For example, a solicitor who did not sympathize with the miners' case nevertheless rejected the notion that the strike was violent, because he had driven past the picket line and had seen what was going on directly. Despite these, and other, evidences of audience activity in relation to the television text, Philo's analysis is still best seen as nearer to the Dominant Text end of the continuum. This is for two reasons. First, and following the earlier work of the Glasgow University Media Group as discussed above, he detects a clear preferred reading in the television presentation of the strike; the television text is not particularly open. As we have already indicated, the reports of the strike were organized around the single issue of violence.

> In practice, our method revealed the 'preferred' meanings of the news. We showed how the repetition of certain views and explanations together with the embracing and underlining of them by journalists were part of a general process by which the news was structured. This was reflected in the choice of material, the themes that were emphasized, the links that were made between these, and the final conclusions that were drawn. (p. 171)

Second, Philo argues that this preferred reading structures the way that the television presentation was received and emerges clearly in what people *remember* one year afterwards. He found a close correspondence between the actual news and the news programmes constructed by his respondents. Some groups were able to reproduce not only the themes of news bulletins on such issues as violence but also the very structure and language of those bulletins. Whatever their attitudes to alleged picket-line violence, the different groups of viewers 'had a relatively uniform understanding of what the television message had been on violence during the miners' strike and on who was portrayed as being responsible for it' (p. 190).

Livingstone (1990) occupies different theoretical ground in a study of television soap opera viewers. In rejecting both Dominant Text and Dominant Audience viewpoints, she sees the creation of meaning through the interaction of texts and readers as a struggle, 'a site of negotiation between *two* semi-powerful sources' (p. 23). What we have is a complex process whereby texts limit what sense viewers can make while themselves being read in widely different ways. In one part of her study, Livingstone showed episodes of *Coronation Street* to a number of viewers. The narrative concerned a father opposing the marriage of his daughter by his first marriage to an older man who had committed adultery with the father's present wife. Livingstone argues that there are two readings potentially available in this narrative. Either true love triumphs over mere prejudice or simple-minded naivety wins over wisdom. A questionnaire was administered to the viewers designed to elicit interpretations of the narrative, and the responses were entered into a cluster analysis. Four clusters of viewers emerged, which Livingstone labels the cynics, the romantics, the negotiated cynics and the negotiated romantics. As the term might imply, the romantics believed that the father was in the wrong, possessive and unreasonable, while the couple were right for each other. The cynics, by contrast, supported the father and did not believe that the couple truly loved each other. The other two clusters occupied positions along the continuum between cynicism and romanticism.

Livingstone next asks the question: what is the relationship between the varied clusters of interpretation and the text; is one of these clusters the dominant reading and one the oppositional? Content analysis of soap opera shows that marriages frequently end in divorce and on the way they are deceitful, unhappy and stressful. As a result, Livingstone suggests that it 'is arguable that, given the nature of soap opera as a genre, the dominant reading inscribed in the text studied here is the cynical reading, with its emphasis on the naivety of young love and the fragility of relationships' (p. 187). On this basis, the romantic reading is an oppositional one. However, at the same time, one could argue that the romantics are effectively endorsing a dominant ideology of romantic love. As Livingstone argues, this shows the complexity of the text–audience relationship. Not only is there a diversity of response to the text, but the most likely explanation of the difficulty of assigning dominant and oppositional labels to the responses is that the text is fragmented and actually contains more than one preferred reading, or, perhaps more precisely, contains a preferred reading which is contradictory.

Further along the continuum from Dominant Text to Dominant Audience lies Fiske's work. In Fiske's (1989a) view, audiences are free to make of television, and popular culture generally, what they will within two major sets of constraints. The first of these is the text itself, while the second is the set of social forces that impinge on audience members and form the attitudes, opinions and beliefs that mould the interpretations that they make of television programmes. What makes Fiske's view distinctive, and closer to the Dominant Audience end of the continuum than any other, is his belief that these constraints are fairly loose, giving more power to the audience:

> People can and do make their own culture, albeit within conditions that are not of their own choosing. How much power is available within this terrain, and how fixedly its boundaries are determined are matters of considerable debate, in which I align myself with those who propose that ideological and hegemonic theories of popular culture have overestimated the power of the determinations and under-estimated that of the viewer. (p. 57)

For Fiske the text is fairly open and polysemic. For example, for television:

> What television delivers is not programs but a semiotic experience. This experience is characterized by its openness and polysemy. Television is not quite a do-it-yourself meaning kit but neither is it a box of ready-made meanings for sale. Although it works within cultural determinations, it also offers freedoms and the power to evade, modify, or challenge these limitations and controls. All texts are polysemic, but polysemy is absolutely central to television's textuality. (p. 59)

At the same time, the analytical attention shifts from the relatively indeterminate text to the audience. And, for Fiske, it is an audience which is very diverse and hence will produce very varied interpretations of media texts. Late capitalist societies are heterogeneous and consist of a vast range of subcultures and groups. The result is that

> Any one person, or television viewer, forms a number of shifting alliances within this heterogeneity, she or he enters the social system via differently constituted and shifting social formations. . . . Any one viewer, then, may at different times be a different viewing subject, as constituted by his or her social determinants, as different alliances may be mobilized for different moments of viewing. (p. 57)

With such an approach to the polysemic text and the diverse audience it is hardly surprising that Fiske takes an extreme view to the point when he declares 'There is no text, there is no audience, there are only the processes of viewing' (p. 57).

Such a view might seem to dissolve the central elements of the IRP. However it is important to note that, however much he may celebrate 'semiotic democracy' (Morley, 1992), Fiske does remain within the paradigm in that the important point is still the relationship of audience response to the unequal distribution of power in a hegemonic order. So he notes that 'popular culture is made in relationship to structures of dominance. This relationship can take two main forms – that of resistance or evasion' (Fiske, 1989b, p. 2). Thus, in a study of the playing of video games in amusement arcades, Fiske (1989b) argues that the players are using the games as a form of resistance in that they are able to assert their own control over the narrative of the game.

In a study of the cultural pursuits of young people, Willis (1990) goes rather further towards the Dominant Audience end of the spectrum. Willis's starting point is in readers not texts and in the need to explore symbolic creativity in everyday life. He argues that all young people are actively carrying out symbolic – cultural – work, not in special and set-aside moments, but in everyday living. Symbolic work is important to the young people con-cerned, and to the wider society, because it produces and repro-duces individual *identities*. In the development of symbolic work the media play an important, if not all-important, role. However, crucially, Willis treats the media, chiefly television, video and music, as *resources* not as *texts*:

> Time and again in our research we were brought back to the perva-siveness of the cultural media in youth experience. The media enter into virtually all of their very creative activities. But whilst the media invite certain interpretations, young people have not only learnt the codes, but have learnt to play with interpreting the codes, to reshape forms, to interrelate the media through their own grounded aesthetics. . . . The meanings they derive from these things inform all their activities. Most importantly, the cultural media are used as a means to vitality, to provide and construct dimensions for what they are and might become. (p. 30)

Television or popular music do not, therefore, function as con-straints on the audience but are instead the raw materials to be used in symbolic work to fashion an identity, a sense of self. Young people use the media; the media do not use young people.

Such a view does not simply construe the audience as active in relation to the text. It goes further and represents the audience as cultural *producers*. For example, in the case of the use of popular music, Willis points to several ways in which his respondents are producers. They engage in home taping, they dance, they operate sound systems and perform with bands. Above all, perhaps, they use the words of songs or the rhythm or beat of music to express their emotions, attitudes and thoughts. They impose their own uses on the raw material provided.

Willis's work provides an extreme example of a Dominant Audience perspective. However, as with Fiske, it is important to stress that it is still (just) within the IRP, while showing the difficulties of maintaining a position within the paradigm. For Willis, the symbolic work carried out by young people is essential to their survival for, especially in the conditions of modern economic life, they are relatively dependent and powerless. Cultural construction here is to be understood in terms of the unequal distribution of power.

So far we have argued that work within the IRP is organized by a concern with the unequal distribution of power within an essentially Marxist model. This is the organizing principle whether the argument is that audiences are constrained by texts or are resistant to them. Much of the work done within the IRP discusses resistance or acquiescence to particular kinds of power relations, especially class relations. Other work treats different forms of power, patriarchal power, for instance. Thus, in her classic study of romance readers, Radway (1987) suggests that the reading of romances both compensates some women for the forms of patriarchal oppression to which they are subject and acts as a form of opposition to that oppression. The primary mechanism of compensation is through escape. Radway argues that the romance readers used this concept in two main ways. First, 'they used the term literally to describe the act of denying the present, which they believe they accomplish each time they begin to read a book and are drawn into its story' (p. 90). Second, 'they used the word in a more figurative fashion to give substance to the somewhat vague but none the less intense sense of relief they experience by identifying with a heroine whose life does not resemble their own in certain crucial aspects' (p. 90).

Reading romances therefore compensates for the nature of the women's own lives and takes them away from them imaginatively. For the women, it is their pleasure, that time in which they can do something for themselves, rather than for their husbands and other members of the family. A similar pattern can be found in Morley's (1986) study of gender and television watching, where women talked of the 'guilty pleasure' of their television watching. For Radway, importantly, this is not just an individualized escape, as she argues that through the reading of romantic fiction women become involved in a wider community of romance readers. She suggests therefore 'that through romance reading the Smithton women are providing themselves with another kind of female community capable of rendering the so desperately needed affective support' (p. 96).

In some respects the escape involved here is through *identification* with the heroine of the story, and hence the readers' preferred novels, which Radway calls the 'ideal romance', are those with a happy ending. Those which do not take this form are seen to be too upsetting and disruptive of escapism and compensation. For Radway, 'romances can be termed compensatory fiction because the act of reading them fulfils certain basic psychological needs for women that have been induced by the culture and its social structures but that often remain unmet in day-to-day existence as the result of concomitant restriction on female activity' (pp. 112–13). To summarize, romance reading compensates in two different ways: first, 'it provides vicarious emotional nurturance by prompting identification between the reader and a fictional heroine whose identity as a woman is always confirmed by the romantic and sexual attentions of an ideal male'; and, second, 'it fills a woman's mental world with the varied details of simulated travel and permits her to converse imaginatively with adults from a broad spectrum of social space' (p. 113).

Radway further argues that this compensation leads to the combating of dominant relations. For her, women's romance reading enables them to refuse the other-directed social role prescribed for them by their position within the institution of marriage. In picking up a book, as they have so eloquently told us, they refuse temporarily their family's otherwise constant demand that they attend to the wants of others even if they act deliberately to do something for their own private pleasure. (p. 211)

Thus, in general, Radway reads romance reading in the frame of incorporation and resistance. Despite their oppositional potential, and their utopian possibility, romances are reactionary and incorporative:

in standing back from this construction of the romance's meaning, once again to assess the implications of the symbolic negation and criticism of the social order, it becomes possible to see that despite the utopian force of the romance's projection, that projection actually leaves unchallenged the very system of social relations whose faults and imperfections gave rise to the romance and which romance is trying to perfect. (p. 215)

In a similar vein, Brown (1994) argues from her study of the way that women talk about soap opera that they use the programmes to express their own dissident attitudes to the power exercised by men. So, *even* if the preferred reading of most soap opera is fundamentally patriarchal, women can still subvert this reading by laughing together about the behaviour of men or by talking together about the way that soap characters are acting as they do because of the powerlessness of women. Brown distinguishes two kinds of pleasure that women take in resistance and which she believes are represented in the soap opera talk that her respondents engaged in. *Active* pleasure for women in soap opera groups

affirms their connection to a women's culture that operates in subtle opposition to dominant culture. It is this culture of the home and of women's concerns, recognized but devalued in patriarchal terms, that provides a notion of identity that values women's traditional expertise. (p. 173)

Reactive pleasure, on the other hand, is one in which a subordinated group recognizes its oppression and reacts to that oppression. Reactive pleasure, while not rejecting the connection women often feel toward women's cultural networks and concerns, also recognizes that these concerns often arise out of women's inability to completely control their own lives. Thus they are able to recognize and feel at an emotional level the price of oppression. (p. 173)

To argue that the IRP is organized around debates about the relationship of audiences and texts to the distribution of power is not to suggest that this is an inappropriate or arbitrary focus. The IRP, indeed, has an entirely plausible set of assumptions at its heart. In essence, it assumes that power relations, especially class relations, are of crucial importance to the operation of society and determine the character of social processes. In making this assumption, the paradigm clearly draws on a long tradition in social theory. It is true that this can be a somewhat mixed tradition. While many writers within the IRP are deploying theories of power which are at least recognizably Marxist, or have been developed out of a debate with Marx's ghost, others are using models that derive from Foucault, Bakhtin or de Certeau. Although these are all theories of power, they can have different theoretical effects. Most importantly, they produce different understandings of the notions of opposition and resistance. For the former, the oppositional readings that might be developed by audiences are *relatively* codified and almost politicized accounts directed at a unified form of power that can be identified by audience members. For the latter, opposition is rather more evasion, a kind of determined unseriousness, a form of play that refuses to take power seriously and is thus undermining. We return to this point later in this and subsequent chapters.

THE GENIE OUT OF THE BOTTLE

As it has been developed, the IRP has manifested a series of stresses and strains which threaten the coherence of the paradigm itself. There have been three main sources of difficulty – the active audience, the gap between empirical studies and the theory of hegemony, and the nature of power and its relationship to commodification.

No theorist of the audience has completely endorsed either the Dominant Text or the Dominant Audience model. As we have already said, these positions represent the ends of a continuum and, over the past twenty or thirty years, media research has see-sawed between them, sometimes emphasizing the activity of the audience and sometimes the powers of the text. As Morley (1989) has said:

> The history of audience studies during the post-war period can be seen as a series of oscillations between perspectives which have stressed the power of the text (or message) over its audiences and perspectives which have stressed the barriers 'protecting' the audience from the potential effects of the message. (p. 16)

There is, however, little doubt that, over the last ten or twenty years, the pendulum has swung more towards the Dominant Audience end of the continuum, by an increasingly heavy emphasis on the idea of the active audience. A great deal of recent work, in that it stresses the diversity of interpretation, the importance of the way that programmes are processed in talk about the media, the skills of the audience in criticizing what they see and hear and the persistent referencing of television to everyday life, embraces a model of the active audience. Buckingham's (1987) study of *EastEnders* could stand for many when he says:

> I shall argue that viewers actively seek to construct their relationship with the programme on their own terms – terms which are often very different from those which appear to be on offer. The meaning of *EastEnders* is not something which is wholly contained within the text, and which is there to be discovered by viewers. On the contrary, it is determined through a process of negotiation between the text and the viewer, in which viewers retain a considerable degree of autonomy to construct their own meanings and pleasures. (p. 154)

Theorists adopting the active audience position have, however, not had the debate all their own way. This is scarcely surprising as a *debate* over whether there is a preferred reading in a text and how active audiences really are in relation to texts constitutes normal science within the paradigm. Three major points are made against those embracing the notion of the active audience by those who are nearer the Dominant Text end of the continuum. First, it is claimed that texts have *some* constraining power and the active audience approach has simply over-emphasized the capacity of audiences to make their own meanings. For example, Curran (1990) argues that television texts are not infinitely open; even if they contain a plurality of meanings, there is definitely one preferred reading and that is bound to limit what audiences can do with the text. Second, there may be a danger of confusing the active audience with the resistant audience. As Cobley (1994) points out, activism does not *of itself* give power or even the capacity to resist. Audiences can be active and give their own meanings to texts without any implication that the preferred meaning of the text is being subverted. Furthermore, even if the preferred reading is subverted by a particular section of the audience, *other* sections of the audience may well have their prejudices confirmed by that preferred reading. Third, in celebrating the activity of the audience, the artistic or moral poverty of the text may be concealed and there is the real danger of a kind of populism in which particular pieces of popular music or particular television programmes must be good just because the audience is active in relation to them.

The critics of the active audience position recognize the potential danger that it poses for the paradigm as a whole. With the emphasis on the active audience, especially when combined with a stress on the polysemic nature of the text, there is a risk that the issue of power will slide off the agenda altogether or, more likely, will be allocated a less central place in the theoretical debate and ensuing empirical work. Such a recognition of the danger is clearly visible in suggestions that strong active audience theories are simply ideologically unsound – a not completely convincing position. Morley (1992), for example, argues:

> The implicit valorization of audience pleasure in this work leads easily into a cultural relativism which, as Curran notes, is readily incorporated into a populist neo-liberal rhetoric which would abandon any concern with cultural values – or 'quality' television (see Brunsdon, 1990) – and functions to justify the positions of the deregulators who would destroy any version of public service broadcasting. As Seiter et al. state pithily, 'in our concern for audiences' pleasures . . . we run the

risk of continually validating Hollywood's domination of the world-wide television market' (Seiter, et al. 1989, p. 5), which certainly would seem to be an odd destination for the trajectory of cultural studies media work. (p. 26)

A solution to the drift promoted by active audience theory is an assertion of the importance of power to an understanding of the relationships between the media and the audience. Morley, in commenting on Fiske's wish to have a theory of the audience which asserts the reader's right to construct readings out of media texts, says:

> While I sympathize with this concern with readers' rights, I would argue that the concept of 'rights' in this context is problematic, in so far as it is perhaps less a question of the readers' rights to make out of a programme whatever meaning they wish . . . than a question of power – for example, the presence or absence of the power or cultural resources necessary to make certain types of meaning . . . . (p. 29)

The difficulty is, however, that, once released, the genie of audience activity is very difficult to cram back in the bottle of the Incorporation/Resistance paradigm and it becomes increasingly difficult to reconcile this activity with a reasonably strong theory of hegemony. Perhaps the extreme of this tendency is revealed in the way that audiences will *play* with media texts. Liebes and Katz (1993) in their study of audiences for *Dallas* found that a section of the audience was given to playful or ludic readings of the serial. Such readings involved 'the trying on of characters, i.e., group members imagining how wonderful or awful it would be to be like them' (p. 190). Interestingly, Liebes and Katz also found that national audiences differed in the extent to which they manifested playful readings. American audiences, in particular, were more inclined to the ludic, which might suggest that the more mature a television audience is, the longer they have had to accustom themselves to the medium, the more likely they are to be able to play with it. Rather more extensively, fans and enthusiasts of the media not only play radically with texts, they actively 'control' them, a point that we take up in more detail in Chapter 5.

In the idea of playful readings any notion of the audience being constrained by the text is starting to disappear. In a sense, therefore, the *ordered* structure given by the IRP is being under-mined by the *disorder* of actual audience response – a disorder of *unpredictability* not of *resistance*. Under these circumstances it is at least worth asking whether it any longer makes theoretical sense to confine audience activity within the framework of incorpora-tion and resistance. Perhaps in very much the same manner as the previous Behavioural paradigm, the IRP is unable to confine the theoretical problems which it itself generates.

The use of Kuhn's notion of paradigm in the study of the natural sciences implies that different paradigms are different ways of looking at the same phenomena. In the social sciences, however, paradigms may change not only because of internal conceptual tensions, but also because of real social changes. In the present case, for example, we have argued that the increasing stress placed on the activity of audiences creates conceptual problems for the IRP. However, the paradigm's theoretical force is also weakened by *changes* in the way that audiences are consti-tuted and in the way that they respond to the rapid proliferation of media texts. In succeeding chapters we will argue that audience members have become much more skilled in their use of the media, and this in itself gives greater capacities to the audience in relation to the text and makes audience responses more diverse and unpredictable. For example, when television began to reach large numbers of people in the 1950s, the medium was rather overwhelming. People did not know how to use it, how to integrate it into their everyday lives. As a result, they fell back on other models of appropriation, drawn from the theatre or cinema, media which demand greater attention (see Press, 1991; Spigel, 1992). Gradually, however, the skill of television use developed, a skill which not only allows very different modes of watching, but is buttressed by greater knowledge of how television is produced and how it achieves its effects. The skilled audience is more likely to be an active audience.

We should also note that tensions within the IRP are enhanced by wider transformations within social theory. In particular, the growing interest in questions of consumption is important. This interest has led to a more positive view of consumption, which is seen no longer as a more or less enforced product of a capitalist economy but as a set of choices made by consumers anxious to construct an identity. This new model of the consumer is isomorphic with the new model of the active audience. Furthermore, one could argue that as audiences are becoming consumers, with the spread of consumer society, so also are consumers becoming audiences, as the provision of images of various kinds, particularly in advertising, becomes more significant in the marketing of consumer goods.

A second major difficulty within the IRP arises from the problem of relating the relatively small-scale conclusions derived from individual empirical studies to the larger-scale social theory of hegemony. The theory underpinning the IRP demands a fair degree of *coherence* in respect both of the texts themselves and of audience responses. It suggests, after all, that texts and audiences – whether they are resistive, accommodative or negotiating – rotate around an axis of power. This is a claim for a *relative* coherence of course; nobody would argue that all texts or audience interpretations had to fall within the framework for the IRP to be sustainable. However, it remains true that most of the work done within the IRP actually tends to show fragmentation rather than coherence. For example, many of the empirical studies within the paradigm are limited in their empirical scope. For television, they are typically based on one text (Wednesday's episode), or series (*Coronation Street*), or genre (soap opera). In any one evening of television watching, however, audiences are exposed to a multitude of texts of radically different formats and genres which do not add up to a coherent experience. Even more diverse, of course, is the audience exposure to the media *as a whole*. An evening's media activity may consist largely of television viewing but at times when there is no suitable programme available, our hypothetical viewer could well listen to Oasis or *La Bohème* and conclude his or her evening by reading the newspaper, a magazine or a book – or all three. Media consumption in the 1990s is essentially a fragmented experience.

If the production and consumption of the media are fragmented now, they are likely to become even more so. In the production of a television programme or record a large number of different elements have to be brought together to create a coherent product.

The achievement of a preferred reading out of a fragmented production process, in other words, requires a great deal of *work*, and that achievement must be persistently vulnerable and insecure. This tendency is greatly enhanced by modern production systems. In a post-Fordist regime of production (see Lash and Urry, 1994), media production systems are splintered amongst a variety of organizations. Even if this does not produce greater diversity at the level of the individual text, it is bound to diversify media production as a whole since the organizational basis for coherence is greatly undermined. At the same time, much recent work on media audiences – to be reviewed in later chapters – indicates that audience responses are becoming more differentiated. In addition, audience responses may also be increasingly *labile* – moving rapidly between different positions over time and between different reception settings. Although there is surprisingly little direct evidence that bears on the question, it is a reasonable hypothesis that audience members will offer different interpretations of the same text depending on who they are with and what purpose is served by the interpretation. Audience readings, in other words, do not constitute some kind of ideological kernel to be carried round and offered up unvaryingly in all situations.

The genie of difference has therefore to be added to the genie of activity. As the IRP has difficulty containing audience activity, so also does it struggle to encompass the fragmentation of media production and reception. This is partly a theoretical difficulty in that it is difficult to unify the diversity of media text and appropriation into the coherent whole demanded by the IRP. It is also an empirical difficulty in that fragmentation and diversification appear to be increasing.

A third difficulty within the IRP concerns the general nature of power and its relationship with culture. As we have already argued, the IRP operates with a particular theory of power which, in turn, suggests that cultural formations are determined in relation to the unequal distribution of power. The assumption within the paradigm is that power is deployed in a relatively unitary way. This assumption is, however, contestable. The arguments come from two different directions. First, there are general theoretical arguments heavily influenced by Foucault, who saw power as contingent, local, fragmented, discontinuous and in a state of flux. Foucault's concern was therefore to ask how power outcomes are achieved out of this flux. The result, as Clegg (1989) notes, is a focus on 'shifting unstable alliances, a concern for military strategy and a disinclination to believe in any single, originating and decisive centre of power' (p. 7).

A second line of argument derives essentially from strains within the paradigm itself. Although much of the empirical work within the IRP focused on resistance or acquiescence to *class* power, more recent work has drawn in other foci of power, particularly those involving gender, age or ethnic difference. The difficulty this creates is that the central assumptions of the IRP become more incoherent and the different axes of power cross-cut each other. One consequence of this is, as Evans (1990) points out, that it becomes difficult to determine what is being resisted and what an oppositional reading would look like. A great deal will depend on context. For example, if some members of a group of women soap opera fans adopt an apparently oppositional reading and some a dominant one, are these readings formed in the context of gender power within the group or within a wider social context which would include men? Or, as Evans puts it,

> Without very careful contextualization, any given reader's variation from other readers (or from what the analyst expects) cannot be labelled as anything but variation. If a particular cultural group, say adolescents, is typified by rebelliousness, then it would be sociologically inconsistent to label a rebellious adolescent reading as oppositional; indeed, given this contextualization, it would be the non-rebellious response that would be resistant. (p. 159)

A related point of view is advanced by Schulze et al. (1993) in their audience study of those who hated Madonna. In their descriptions of the views of Madonna haters, these authors point to four critical accounts of Madonna: as the lowest form of culture, as 'the lowest form of irresponsible culture, a social disease'; 'the lowest form of the feminine'; and 'as the antithesis of feminism'. They report that these readers of Madonna feel that they are going against the dominant ideas of Madonna as a 'good thing', and that they are, in the phrase of Schulze et al., 'resistive readers'. They argue that is the opposite of how resistant or resistive readers are normally conceptualized. Thus, they suggest that resistive readings such as these tend to be ignored. 'The danger in disqualifying readings such as theirs as dominant readings is that it too easily permits overly romanticized notions that audiences of popular culture always valiantly resist dominant ideology in progressive ways' (p. 32).

Such arguments as these undermine the central assumptions of the IRP concerning the way that power is organized in modern society. If power is indeed diffused, and is not exercised in a unitary way on behalf of a dominant power bloc, then it makes *less* sense to see the culture of a society as driven by the twin forces of domination and resistance. Encounters with the media then become just that – relatively more isolated events not conducted within a unitary framework of domination.

ANOTHER PARADIGM?

If the IRP is beginning to break up, is there an alternative paradigm that would see audiences not as resistant or acquiescent, but in some other way, perhaps by *not* treating audiences as being *addressed*? We will argue in succeeding chapters that there is an emerging paradigm which we shall refer to as the Spectacle/ Performance paradigm (henceforth the SPP) which is based on rather different assumptions. The SPP may be partly produced by the theoretical and empirical difficulties of the IRP to which we have referred. Crucially, however, the SPP is a response to changes in the nature of the audience and in the experience of being a member of an audience. These changes are produced by a number of factors. The process of commodification, for instance, begins to treat individuals simultaneously as consumers and as members of an audience. Or, again, people's pastimes and hobbies are increasingly constructed as events in which the participants are more like members of an audience. The net effect of these processes and others is that the qualities and experiences of being a member of an audience have begun to *leak out* from specific performance

	1 Behavioural	2 Incorporation/ Resistance	3 Spectacle/ Performance
Audience	Individuals (in social context)	Socially structured (e.g. by class, gender, race)	Socially constructed and reconstructed especially by spectacle and narcissism
Medium	Stimulus (message)	Text	Mediascape(s)
Social consequence(s)	Functions/ dysfunctions, propaganda, influence, use, effects	Ideological incorporation and resistance	Indentity formation and reformation in everyday life
Representative studies and approaches	'Effects' literature, uses and gratifications	Encoding and decoding, Morley (1980), Radway (1987) fans studies	Silverstone (1994), Hermes (1995), Gillespie (1995)

FIGURE 1.1   *The three paradigms*

events which previously contained them, into the wider realms of everyday life. Being a member of an audience becomes a mundane event. For this reason, the SPP foregrounds the notion of identity; being a member of an audience is intimately bound up with the construction of the person. Figure 1.1 summarizes some of the differences between the three paradigms which are discussed in the next two chapters.

It is important to note that the SPP does not simply controvert the central claims of the IRP, and, given that the former has evolved out of the latter, the two paradigms will have a great deal in common. What it does is to assign an inferior place to the theoretical problem of the IRP and replace it with another around which research can take place. It is not therefore that power is irrelevant to the SPP, but only that it is not the central element. The relationship between the central problems of the two paradigms, and particularly between identity and power, is an important question to which we will return.

2

Forms of the Audience

The essence of the Spectacle/Performance paradigm by comparison with the Incorporation/Resistance paradigm is a redefinition of what an audience *is* and what it *does*. In this chapter we explore these issues by contrasting three types of audience experience – the simple audience, the mass audience and the diffused audience.

In contemporary societies all three types of audience experience are present. Pre-modern societies, on the other hand, manifest only simple audiences. It is therefore important to note that the distinction between simple, mass and diffused audiences is both synchronic and diachronic. We will want to argue that mass and diffused audiences develop out of simple audiences, created by the forces of modernization, but do not replace them.

In the previous chapter, we identified some difficulties with the IRP, some of which are generated internally within the paradigm while others are produced – 'externally' to the paradigm – by changes in the way that audiences behave. The distinction between simple, mass and diffused audiences gives a different way of looking at the internal and external stresses within these paradigms. The IRP is particularly suitable for the analysis of simple audiences and, to some extent, of mass audiences. It has some difficulty in coping with diffused audiences, however, and even more with the contemporary complex relationship between all three audience types existing simultaneously. The SPP, on the other hand, is more at home with the diffused audience.

PERFORMANCE

Critical to what it means to be a member of an audience is the idea of *performance*. Audiences are groups of people before whom a performance of one kind or another takes place. Performance, in turn, is a kind of activity in which the person performing accentuates his or her behaviour under the scrutiny of others. That accentuation is deliberate, even if unconscious. It is 'behaviour heightened, if ever so slightly, and publicly displayed; twice-behaved behaviour' (Schechner, 1993, p. 1). This 'heightening' gives a certain tension to the performance and its reception by an audience. As Turner (1982) has pointed out, performance involves a relationship between performer and audience in which a liminal space, however slight, is opened up. The performer–audience interaction occurs within, or represents, critical areas in which a society is self-reflexive; it provides a kind of window, 'a limited area of transparency', through which an examination of socially and culturally sensitive issues is possible. Any performance therefore carries with it some sense of specialness, a moment of being transported out of the mundane, even if the transportation is brief and slight.

As we will argue later, performances are clearly of various different kinds and, as a result, audiences are found in a variety of circumstances and events. The theatre is perhaps the archetypical instance, a live event in which the architecture of the setting (with some deliberate exceptions) emphasizes the distinction between performers and audience. We, in common with many other authors (for example, Chaney, 1993; Schechner, 1985, 1988, 1993; Turner, 1982, 1986) want to extend the notions of performers and audiences much further than this to other quite different settings. As Schechner (1988) says:

> Performance is an inclusive term. Theater is only one node on a continuum that reaches from the ritualizations of animals (including humans) through performances in everyday life – greetings, displays of emotion, family scenes, professional roles, and so on – through to play, sports, theater, dance, ceremonies, rites, and performances of great magnitude. (p. xii)

Religious worship, political meetings, sports events, concerts, television and radio programmes all fairly clearly have performers and audiences. Public rituals and ceremonies such as funerals, carnivals, and processions also fall into the category. Less obvious are those events, going to a picture gallery for example, where the performers are not present to the degree that they are in the theatre. Less obvious still is the sphere of everyday life which some writers say is constituted by performance. All of these instances can usefully be treated as performance–audience interactions. At the same time, the rules governing those interactions do vary between different types of performance event and it is those rules that distinguish the three different types of audience experience, simple, mass and diffused. Before we come to a more detailed account of the types of audience experience, we need to identify a number of closely connected characteristics of performances and audiences in general.

All performances involve a degree of ceremony and ritual (and ceremonies require performance, as we indicated above). Going to the theatre is a ceremonial event. The audience may dress relatively formally, the play is received in silence, the rules of behaviour are fairly circumscribed. It would be tempting to see performances in the mass media as somehow lacking this ritual quality. However, as we shall argue later, even the act of watching television or listening to a record at home can have elements of ceremony. In turn, all performances, though to very different degrees, will be invested with a sense of the sacred and the extraordinary. Religious worship is an obvious example, though perhaps atypical. Many political meetings are imbued with the sense that something out of the ordinary is going on, something that transcends everyday life and is not part of it. We have to stress again that qualities of sacredness are attributed to performances in very different ways and to very different degrees. The act of listening to recorded music while washing up is clearly less extraordinary and more profane than attending a concert of the very same music.

The qualities of sacredness and ceremony attached to performances are clearly connected with the distance – physical and social – between performer and audience. Performance spaces separate audience and performer and the physical separation is, of course, more pronounced in the case of the mass media. The sense of *social* distance is, however, even more important. As a rule, performers acquire a mystique which separates them from the ordinary lives of the audience. They are a separate order of beings inhabiting an extra-mundane world.

Performance spaces are important for other reasons. The archetypical performances of the theatre are conducted in *public* spaces and it is this public appearance which is responsible for the ceremonial and sacred qualities that are attached to the performances. Appearance in public requires, for most of the time at least, a measure of decorum and restraint. Public spaces are more conventionalized and rule-bound than are private ones. At the same time, private spaces, because they are necessarily associated with the everyday, routine measures of ordinary life, are *relatively* more hostile to ceremonial conduct. It is important to note the obvious point, however, that not all performances are held in public. The advent of the mass media, indeed, successfully privatizes performance; reception of television, radio or recorded music is largely domestic. The idea of performance in the mass media is clearly a somewhat slippery one. There is the original performance that is recorded and transmitted but the reception of that performance, probably at a different time and place, is, in a sense, another performance before a different audience. This difference between a primary and a secondary performance was clearer in the early history of the mass media than it is at the end of the twentieth century. For example, much recorded music on disc was literally a recording of a traditional concert before an audience. For classical music that is still the case to some extent. Recorded popular music, although not dependent on a concert on the whole, did use the conventions of live performance to some extent until fairly recently. Artists would perform a song all the way through *as if* they were performing live. More recently, however, recording conventions have changed and parts of songs are spliced together to make a whole that has never been performed. The importance of the original event, the primary performance, has therefore declined in relation to the secondary performance which takes place in the private domestic setting. Mass media performances are therefore *increasingly* privatized.

Performances not only take place in public or private spaces but can also be seen as localized or globalized. Hence the live performance is conducted in a limited physical space. Mass media performances, on the other hand, are not so localized. Depending on the limits of language and cultural convention, they are regional, national or global.

When members of an audience people *attend* to a performance, they concentrate their energies, emotions and thoughts on the performance and try to distil from that performance a meaning of one kind or another. Commonsensically, it seems likely that attention is related to involvement and involvement is related to effect. That is to say, the more intense the audience attention, the more involved it will be in the performance and the greater will be the intellectual and emotional impact. But the capacity of the audience to give attention, and to become involved, will vary over time, by the type of performance, and by the medium by which the performance is transmitted. The theatre is a high-attention medium and television is typically low-attention. This general characterization, however, obscures the way in which audiences for these two media can switch from high to low attention and back again during performances depending on all sorts of factors, including the ceremonial quality of the setting and its relative privacy.

We develop this discussion of the characteristics of performance in the following sections and in the subsequent chapters. The argument will be that performance is central to the construction of audiences and that different modes of performance are related to different types of audience experience. Figure 2.1 summarizes this argument.

THE SIMPLE AUDIENCE

On the face of it, the audience is relatively easy to define. The *Shorter Oxford English Dictionary* defines it as 'The persons within hearing' (coming from the Latin root) and suggests that in the

	Simple	Mass	Diffused
Communication	Direct	Mediated	Fused
Local/Global	Local	Global	Universal
Ceremony	High	Medium	Low
Public/Private	Public	Private	Public and Private
Distance	High	Very high	Low
Attention	High	Variable	Civil inattention

FIGURE 2.1   *Modes of audience experience*

mid-nineteenth century this usage was transferred to the readers of a book. This definition suggests a certain immediacy in the experience of being a member of an audience. There is a communication of some kind between a sender and a receiver, this communication is fairly direct, the context is spatially localized and, typically, takes place in a public space. There is a reasonably clear distinction between producers and consumers: producers perform and audiences appropriate the performance with a great deal of attention and involvement. Events involving simple audiences of this kind are exceptional, depend on a certain ceremonial quality, and demand relatively high levels of attention and involvement. They are not, in other words, the stuff of everyday life. Performances to simple audiences are *noticed*. They involve extensive preparation on the part of the performers (rehearsal, the construction of performance spaces) *and* of the audience (making arrangements to go, dressing). There is also usually an aftermath in that performaces will be discussed or even written about.

Examples of simple audiences with these characteristics include those who attend concerts, plays, films, festivals, political meetings, public celebrations, carnivals, funerals, legal trials, religious events and football matches. Although these are all examples of simple audiences, they are, of course, also very different from one another. The theatrical or aesthetic performances clearly have their own specific and peculiar rules which will differ from those organizing performances in sport or public rituals, for example.

Simple audiences participate in performance events which have a substantial ceremonial or sacred quality. Clearly religious worship, observances or festivals have ritual, sacred or ceremonial elements and these are common to Eastern and Western faiths. Courtrooms similarly are the settings for performances imbued with substantial ceremony. The rules of behaviour are well marked, there is a pervasive sense of etiquette, the language is formal, and the major actors are costumed. The theatre, too, is ceremonial.

> The lights go up; the actors appear; the performance begins. It is a multiple creation – the outcome of the dramatist's purpose, the producer's style, the actors' performances and the audience's participation. But first and foremost it is a *ceremony*.
> Everything contributes to the ceremonial aspect of the theatre – the solemnity of the place, the separation between a secular audience and a group of actors isolated in a restricted, illuminated world, the actors' costumes, their precise gestures and the specificity of a poetic language which proclaims a basic distinction between the language of the theatre and everyday conversation. (Duvignaud, 1965, p. 82)

In this context it is worth noting how the early theatre was bound up with religious observance, giving a sacred element to performance almost automatically. Attendance at festivals of drama in ancient Greece, for example, was primarily to honour Dionysus. There were similar intimate connections between worship and drama in medieval Europe. Alongside the Mass and during the Christian festivals at Easter and Christmas, there would be small dramatic presentations to accompany the more formal worship. At the same time, performances outside the street depended on Bible stories. The trade guilds in particular would use such stories for the plays that they put on each year.

One of the clearest expressions of contemporary ritual and ceremony can be found in sports events and the audiences that attend them. For example, many commentators have drawn attention to the almost religious nature of football. Perhaps the most well-known football quote of all time came from the late Bill Shankly, when, as manager of Liverpool, he opined that football was a more important matter than life or death – a sentiment which Murphy et al. (1990) recognize as coming 'close to capturing the quasi-religious character of the support that the game manages to attract in countries all over the world' (p. 1). Edgell and Jary (1973) make the argument more sociologically when they suggest that 'Football expands from a private inter-group game to become, what many see as, a kind of theatre or surrogate religion. A team's supporters become members of communities of shared experience, values, and above all, shared emotionalism' (p. 221).

The ritualistic and ceremonial quality of performances to simple audiences of all kinds is not accidental of course. Schechner (1988), for example, believes that there is a kind of dialectical process whereby theatre turns into ritual and, conversely, ritual is formed by theatre. There is a constant flow from one to the other and back again.

> The move from ritual to theatre happens when a participating audi-
> ence fragments into a collection of people who attend because the
> show is advertised, who pay admission, who evaluate what they are
> going to see before, during, and after seeing it. The move from theatre
> to ritual happens when the audience is transformed from a collection
> of separate individuals into a group or congregation of participants.
> (p. 142)

Avant-garde theatre companies, in Schechner's view, try to move towards the ritual pole by encouraging audience participation and greater integration of performances, and performance spaces, in local communities. Other writers go further in arguing that it is not simply that theatre and ritual are connected, but also that the connexion between the two is based on the functions that theatre performs in society. Turner (1986), for example, argues that ritualistic performances, whether religious or not, whether conducted in simple societies or complex ones, are *liminal*; they constitute a threshold between secular living and sacred living. They take place in separate spaces and at separate times, set off from times and places otherwise reserved for work, food and sleep. At the same time the experience of ritual does not leave its participants unchanged.

> Rituals separated specified members of a group from everyday life,
> placed them in a limbo that was not any place they were in before and
> yet any place they would be in, then returned them, changed in some
> way, to mundane life. (p. 25)

As with rituals strictly interpreted, so also with theatre. In modern societies theatrical performances have many of the characteristics of ritual, and, for Turner, also have many of the same functions. Precisely because of its liminality, theatrical performance enables a society to look at itself. It can 'probe a community's weaknesses, call its leaders to account, desacralize its most cherished values and beliefs, portray its characteristic conflicts and suggest remedies for them, and generally take stock of its current situation in the known "world"' (Turner, 1982, p. 11, quoted in Bennett, 1997, p. 105). In creating the conditions for a societal self-reflexivity, theatre also provides the means for handling social conflict, thus having a function similar to that provided by religious and other rituals.

Ceremony implies a certain physical and social *distance* between performers and audience. Except in avant-garde theatrical forms, of which more in a moment, there is a physical separation between actors and audience and the rare moments when the performers do descend into the auditorium can produce a sense of awkwardness in the audience. This separation is even more marked in political and sports events in which any intermingling of performer and spectator is treated as a breach of security. It is important to note here that physical and social separation is a historical achievement. Earlier dramatic performances were relatively informal and 'contact between actors and audiences was immediate and intimate' (Williams, 1970, p. 33). But, as Burns (1972) notes, 'The process of separation between actors and spectators was more or less completed in England by the time the first full-time theatre (*The Theater*) was built in 1576' (p. 348). Increasingly, over the next three hundred years, theatrical settings became more formal, further emphasizing the separation between actors and audiences.

One can note a similar physical distance between audience and performer in other instances, such as the courtroom, football matches and political meetings. Commonsensically, this physical separation seems almost intrinsic to the whole notion of performance. In some ways more interesting, therefore, is the *social* distance between performers and simple audiences. For example, at funerals conducted in church, members of the family of the deceased are almost invariably physically separated from the rest of the congregation by being placed close to the minister. But this physical separation is reinforced by a sense of ritual distance between family and other mourners. They are in a separate category because their loss is assumed to be, by orders of magnitude, greater than that of anyone else. Their grief, and the necessary transformations of their social status, makes them temporarily into members of a different order of being. Physical and social distance makes members of the family into performers in the ritual, a feature illustrated, as so often, in the liminal or marginal case.

This discussion of social distance raises issues of the distinctions and divisions in the simple audience. We shall consider the segmentation of contemporary audiences in more detail in Chapter 5. However, at this point, it can be suggested that as simple audiences develop over time, status differences (which were reflected in price) tend to become replaced by differences based more centrally on price alone. For example, divisions in theatre and especially cinema audiences between front and back stalls and circle, which were common, have now been almost completely eliminated by a system of unified pricing, where the possibility of obtaining the best seat is dependent on either arriving early to book a seat or doing the same by credit card. Such processes of de-differentiation, commodification and consumerization have also occurred very recently in the simple audience at Premier League football matches. Thus, while there are still distinctions between parts of the ground, these are now based much more on price. All spectators have seats and the divisions between terraces, enclosures and stands have been removed.

The social separation of performers and audiences is reinforced by the manner in which the former inhabit an extra-mundane world. In the theatre, this social distance derives from the social status of actors. In the early theatre, actors were mere journeymen and were socially close to the audience. By the seventeenth century, however, their social status was much improved and some actors were accepted into fashionable society. By the late nineteenth and twentieth centuries the profession has become almost respectable to the point at which it seems perfectly natural that actors will be given knighthoods and even peerages. More significant than an improving social status in creating social distance between actor and audience, however, is the manner in which actors partake in the *aura* of the performance. As Benjamin (1970) puts it: 'The aura which, on the stage, emanates from Macbeth cannot be separated for the spectators from that of the actor' (p. 231).

It is possible to trace changes in the nature of footballers and their construction as stars in a similar manner. Thus, Critcher (1979) identifies a movement in the period since the Second World War through four styles of hero: the 'traditional/located', 'transitional/mobile', 'incorporated/embourgeoised' to the 'superstars/dislocated'. Critcher argues that the first type of hero 'represents and draws on the values of a traditional respectable working-class culture' and was exemplified by the heroes of the immediate post-war period such as Stanley Matthews, Nat Lofthouse, Tom Finney and so on. These heroes tended to remain at their home-town club and to in some sense represent it. The transitional figures who began to explore some of the new experiences offered by increased remuneration and so on are represented by players like Bobby Charlton – in Critcher's view 'a working-class gentleman who could live like one' (p. 165), and was pre-eminent in the early 1960s. When footballers became 'incorporated and embourgeoised', 'they became small-scale entrepreneurs, a world away from their predecessors and most of their contemporary supporters' (p. 164). The image, according to Critcher, was of the small businessman. The superstar arrived in the late 1960s with George Best, whose story 'should be read in wider cultural terms, as the biography of a dislocated footballing hero, whose talent, personality and background were insufficient to withstand the pressures, both on and off the field, to which the new type of superstar was to be subjected' (p. 167). By the 1970s the new heroes were able to cope with these pressures. A similar history and argument can be made about the rock stars of the late 1960s and early 1970s whose lives ended tragically (Joplin, Jones, Hendrix, Morrison, and so on) in contrast to rock stars of the 1980s and 1990s, such as Phil Collins and Madonna, who can deal with the life of the superstar.

In general terms what is traced here is an increase in social distance as the star becomes removed from the community from which he or she is initially located. Importantly, in the contemporary period such stardom and distance is managed through star texts (see Goodwin, 1993) which construct and reconstruct the star's image through various publications along a number of different lines of narrative. It is possible to speculate that the contemporary star text of a player such as Alan Shearer, who became the most expensive footballer in the world when transferred from Blackburn Rovers to Newcastle United in the summer of 1996, owes much to the construction of him as the respectable working class male made good, combining elements of the working-class populism of a Bruce Springsteen with the clean-cutness of a Bobby Charlton, on a reported wage (note not salary) of £30,000 per week. Shearer's move was widely reported as motivated by his desire to play for his home-town club.

One of the effects of the distance between performers and audience is the creation of an apparent audience passivity. As already indicated above, in the theatre this passivity is historically relatively new. Greek theatre involved the audience symbolically, architecturally and in the conduct of the performance. 'Medieval and sixteenth-century audiences did not enjoy the power of the Greek audiences, but nevertheless still functioned in an active role. There was flexibility in the relationship between stage and audience worlds which afforded, in different ways, the participation of those audiences as actors in the drama' (Bennett, 1997, p. 3). The whole tone and feel of the theatrical experience was different, as Bradbrook (1962, p. 97, quoted in Carlson, 1996, p. 84) notes: 'The theatre of the Elizabethans, in its social atmosphere, was less like the modern theatre than it was like a funfair. . . . Merriment, jigs, and toys followed the performance: songs, dumb shows, fights, clowns' acts were interlaced.' Sennett (1977) notes the connexions in the eighteenth-century theatre between the physical and social distance between audience and performers, audience passivity and apparent audience enjoyment. Earlier in the century, although those of higher rank sat during the performance, those of middling rank more usually stood and held conversations and ate food. Some members of the audience sat on the stage and were almost part of the action in that they would stroll across the stage or wave to friends whenever the mood took them. At the same time, audiences participated in the drama, displaying extremities of emotion in response to events on stage or testing the actors as they spoke their lines. Gradually, however, audiences became motionless, as they were all seated, more passive and more bourgeois. The noisy, even riotous behaviour of working-class audiences turned into the sedate passivity of the middle class. Audiences do not participate in the spectacle except in certain limited and predefined ways, clapping and cheering, for example. A kind of social contract is entered into by the audience. 'With this social contract put into place, usually by the exchange of money for a ticket which promises a seat in which to watch an action unfold, the spectator accepts a passive role and awaits the action which is to be interpreted' (Bennett, 1997, p. 204). As Kershaw (1994) points out, the very physical arrangements and conventions of the theatre imply a certain fixity for the audience:

> As with cinema, to gain access to the performance we agree to be channelled through an ever more limiting physical regime, until we are seated to focus within a narrow angle of vision, normally to remain there for a period we do not determine. Moreover, once the live actors begin their work, the audience is under a greater injunction than can ever occur in the cinema. Anyone who has been compelled to leave a live performance during its course will know what constraining forces are built into the conventions created for its consumption. (p. 176)

This strong sense of propriety/passivity is manifested in other simple audience performances. Atkinson (1984), for example, shows clearly what a skilled performance speaking at political meetings is. Good speakers are as accomplished as actors in their sense of timing, their ability to draw applause at the appropriate moment, and their general capacity to control their audiences. The audiences at such meetings, on the other hand, are relatively passive and there is a strong sense of what behaviour is permissible. For Atkinson, the rule-bound nature of simple audiences is amply illustrated by the discomfort felt when one does something wrong.

> It is the sort of experience that will be familiar to anyone who has ever stood up just at the point in a church service when the rest of the congregation knelt down, or who has started clapping at a concert after the fourth movement of what subsequently turned out to be a five-movement symphony. When we are seen to step out of line, we draw attention to our ignorance of how to behave properly on such occasions, and may find our social competence called into question. (p. 18)

Atkinson also points out that special means may be adopted to ensure that an audience behaves as one body. For example, across a very wide range of public gatherings, from church services to football matches, music is used to provide a rhythmic beat which enables thousands of individuals to join in and act as one body.

As with the development of theatre noted above, passivity is a historical development. Political meetings, as late as the nineteenth century, were rowdy affairs in which the audience was anything but passive. In the sense that visiting an art gallery may be treated as a performance event, in the nineteenth century such visitors were expected to be active, studying what they saw to the point of sketching it rather than simply scanning the entire collection. Much the same point could be made for the development of sporting events. Furthermore, the more participant and least properly behaved simple audiences in contemporary society are drawn from social groups that are defined as lacking in the 'civilized' virtues – the young at rock concerts and the working class at football matches. The point has been made by the researchers on football commonly known as the 'Leicester' School, in accord with the general arguments of Elias, that 'football hooliganism' in Britain in the 1970s and 1980s could be explained by the way in which society had moved in a more civilized direction, leaving socially unacceptable some forms of behaviour that would previously have been tolerated.

It is important that many contemporary developments in football could be said to be turning a crowd more clearly into a simple audience, in a way similar to the example of the theatre discussed above. Thus, until the recent advent of all-seat stadia, a significant proportion of the crowd would have been standing up, and, until the development of segregation of spectators as a control measure, would have had almost complete freedom of movement from one area of the ground to another. For example, movement of fans from one end of the ground to another was common at many matches in the 1960s and it was possible to stand behind the goal being attacked by the team supported for all of the match. Contemporary Premier League football is far more regulated. All audience members are seated in a designated place, with very little access to other sections of the ground. Some areas of seating are non-smoking, and so on. It is clear that there is potentially developing social pressure not to move from the designated seat during the course of the match, mainly because it will have the effect of obscuring the view of others – a phenomenon previously experienced at the theatre and cinema. Of course, in earlier periods it was actually rather difficult to move at a game, where the crowd was so densely populated.

One effect of this seating and regulation of the audience is a focus on the game itself. This may seem absurd, as what else would the crowd focus on? However, it can be suggested that an important element in the crowd was the interaction amongst audience members themselves; this is now much more difficult, on both the physical and verbal planes. We do not suggest that this has been eliminated, rather that there are different patterns of behaviour and interaction developing, which take football closer to a simple audience of the theatrical type. This process has been widely recognized among football fans and professionals. Thus, during the 1996/7 season, the manager of Manchester United, Alex Ferguson, complained that the crowd at Old Trafford were simply waiting to be entertained, rather than actively supporting the team in the 'traditional' way. There is much talk of turning the crowd into an audience, and there was much shaking of heads among football fans about the fan of Manchester United who contacted a radio phone-in programme to argue that the reason for purchasing a ticket to a game was not to see the team she supported lose.

The notion of audience passivity should, however, be treated with some caution. In the case of the theatre, for example, whatever it means, it does not necessarily imply that the theatre is a low-attention/low-involvement medium. Quite the reverse: theatre audiences are giving high attention to the spectacle and, partly as a consequence, are closely involved. As Bennett (1997) puts it: 'Spectators are thus trained to be passive in their demonstrated behaviour during a theatrical performance, but to be active in their decoding of the sign systems made available. Performers rely on the active decoding, but passive behaviour of the audience so that they can unfold the planned on-stage activity' (p. 206). By contrast with mass audiences (see the next section), the circumstances in which simple audiences are found are designed to concentrate attention on the spectacle and make it impossible to carry on other activities at the same time. As Atkinson (1984) makes clear, skilled orators employ a number of techniques to make sure that their audience attends to what they are saying. Audience inattention is a permanent risk in public speaking, which, after all, involves prolonged speech which no member of the audience can interrupt, features unusual in everyday conversation. So, good speakers will make sure that they look round their audience, keep it under surveillance, since it will be embarrassing for anyone to be caught out not attending. They will be successful in getting the audience to register approval and will combine 'a variety of carefully co-ordinated verbal, non-verbal, intonational, and rhythmic signals in the production of an invitation to applaud' (Atkinson, 1984, p. 121).

Theatre audience members, similarly, are expected not to make a noise or to converse, and it would be profoundly odd – or even offensive – if people attending a concert or sports event were to be found reading a book. In other words, the performance conventions for simple audiences demand high attention. The reactions of other audience members reinforce that convention, as will be made clear to those who unwrap toffees or chat during a concert, a political speech or a funeral. Such reinforcement need not be provided at the time. For example, the disdain with which sports, concert and theatre enthusiasts greet the tendency of businesses to use performances to entertain their clients indicates the power of the convention that, in attending performances in these areas, one is expected to concentrate on the concert, play, horse-race or cricket match and not be diverted by engaging in other, irrelevant, activities.

Simple audiences inhabit localized – and often specialized – spaces which often lie unused for long periods of time when there is no performance. When used, however, the use is intensive. The spaces all have the capacity to allow a relatively large group of people to watch and hear a relatively small group. At the same time the performance is confined to those within earshot or range of vision; the space makes possible an *unmediated* performance. All these features enhance the ceremonial and celebratory aspects of simple audience performances that we noted earlier. They allow, encourage, demand a *condensed*, intense experience.

Simple audience spaces can themselves be treated as sacred. An important example of this is the football ground. As Edgell and Jary (1973) point out, 'Grounds can certainly possess the aura of a church' (p. 224), and Taylor's (1989) reflections on the Hillsborough disaster make much of the meanings attached to the ground on his part. As Taylor notes, in the aftermath of the disaster both Hillsborough and Anfield were turned into shrines, where wreaths and memorabilia of all kinds were left in tribute by fans. It might be thought that the 'audiencing' of football could lead to a decline in the sense of connexion to the ground as a kind of sacred place, especially as some areas of ground more closely resemble the anonymous spaces of the shopping mall. However, some evidence seems to suggest that pride in the ground is still an important dimension of football attachment. Thus, King (1995), in his work on Manchester United supporters, argues that one dimension of attack of the other local club, Manchester City, was of its ground and the 'manifest' cheapness of its new stand.

It is also worth noting the obvious fact that the performance spaces for simple audiences are invariably *public*. On occasions, access to such spaces is limited. By convention, attendance at funerals and weddings, for example, is by invitation. However, even in these cases, it is perfectly proper for the uninvited to turn up even if they are not prominent members of the audience. For the bulk of simple performance events, however, there are no such restrictions other than the ability to pay. For those events conducted in municipal spaces – parks, squares or streets – even that limitation does not apply. For many types of simple audience performance, the fact that performance is in public is of crucial importance. Political theatre, which shades off into public political demonstrations, for example, achieves its effect by contesting with the authorities the use of public space. As Schechner (1993) points out, whether it is street theatre protesting against the Vietnam War or demonstrations against the Berlin Wall or in Tiananmen Square, the essence of the performance is to create a dissident disorder against the order of conventional and authoritative use. Authorities use public space for regular and ordered processions; dissidents disrupt that set of expectations. As Jerry Rubin said: 'Life is theatre and we are the guerrillas attacking the shrines of authority . . . the street is the stage' (Rubin, 1970, p. 250, quoted in Schechner, 1993, p. 64).

Avant-garde theatre groups have a particular interest in getting and maintaining the audience's attention and, in doing so, may deliberately ignore some of the other features of simple audience performances that we have been describing. In particular, they wish to have an active and participant audience, to break down the barriers between audience and performers, to eliminate some codes of polite behaviour and to use public spaces for performance. Boal (1979), for instance, argues for a theatre that departs from both Aristotelian and Brechtian practice. Aristotelian theatre imposes its world on passive spectators, who are unable to think outside the categories presented and are therefore also unable to act. Brechtian theatre goes one step further in that it deliberately fosters a critical stance on the part of the audience but it still denies the capacity for action, giving that to the characters instead. As Boal says:

> In the beginning the theater was the dithyrambic song: free people singing in the open air. The carnival. The feast.
>
> Later, the ruling classes took possession of the theater and built their dividing walls. First they divided the people, separating actors from spectators: people who act and people who watch – the party is over! Secondly, among the actors, they separated the protagonists from the mass. The coercive indoctrination began! (p. 119)

In order that audiences will engage with the performance, it is important, above all, that the social and physical distance between the two be lessened or eliminated. In a study of the audience of a bilingual theatre group in Australia, Shevstova (1992) notes the way in which there are a very large number of performers, some of whom are simply local residents. The show started in a park, became a procession through the streets, and finally filled a school. The use of these public spaces effectively lessened the distance between performers and audience. Shevstova's survey of the audience shows that, as a result of this type of performance, the audience demonstrates that 'they are not mere spectators either of their own lives or of stage performances. They assert their will to act upon their collective existence and, in doing so, show they are protagonists of their society' (p. 117). Furthermore, the forms that subsequently became known as 'performance art' break down more than the barriers between audience and performer (Carlson, 1996). In particular the distinction between art and everyday life is dissolved and the focus of performance is as much on 'spectacle' as it is on 'text'. These are features of performance to what we will call 'diffused audiences', to which we return for a more detailed discussion later.

To recapitulate, the main features of the simple audience are that: communication between performers and the audience is direct; the performance event takes place at a designated, 'local' place; the event is invested with a high degree of ceremony by the audience; the performance is public; the distance between the audience and the event is high; as, finally, is the attention of the audience.

MASS AUDIENCES

Pre-modern societies, with an extensive dependence on an orally transmitted culture, largely operated with simple audiences. It is often argued that the advent of mass communications, particularly radio, television, recorded music and film, has removed the support for simple audience performances. It might therefore be said that film has ruined theatre, the art of public speaking is dead, people no longer attend religious or other public ceremonies, and the technology of recorded music has made the live concert obsolete. These arguments are misleading. Simple audiences are as important, if not more important, in contemporary society than in pre-modern ones. Audiences for theatre, concerts, political meetings, church services and other varieties of simple audience performances continue to be large and may well be even larger than they were in earlier times.

However, equally obviously, the arrival of systems of mass communications has had an impact on the experience of being a member of an audience. Watching the television, listening to a CD or the radio, reading a newspaper or magazine, are manifestly different kinds of experience from going to a play. A great deal has been written about the characteristics of the mass media and mass audiences (see, for example, Giner, 1976; McQuail, 1987; Thompson, 1995). Attention has focused on such topics as: the standardization of communication; the commodification of the media; the impersonality of communication; the mediocrity and vulgarity of mass media content; the institutionalization of the whole process of performance and communication; the extension of symbolic forms in space and time; and the public sphere nature of mass media transmission as opposed to reception. We are going to concentrate on the nature of the relationship between audience and performance. Accordingly, by comparison with performances to simple audiences, mass audience events do not involve spatial localization, the communication is not so direct, the experience is more of an everyday one and is not invested in quite the same way with ceremony, less attention is paid to the performance, which is typically received in private rather than public, and there is even greater social and physical distance between performers and audience. These changes justify one speaking of a *mass audience*. However, it is also worth noting that mass audiences and simple audiences also have a good deal in common. They both depend on *performance* and, crucially, they both involve a communication between producers and consumers who are kept physically and socially separate from one another. Indeed, as we shall show later, it is important to note that performances to simple and mass audiences flow into one another, can be dependent on one another, and are even parasitic on one another. At times, of course, this can be a simple matter of the mass transmission of performances to simple audiences, as in the case of concerts, political meetings and even church services. These are relatively rare, however, and more significant are those events that are performances, even if not in the conventional sense, which are picked up by the mass media. For example, political theatre in the widest sense, against the Vietnam War or Greenpeace's action against French nuclear tests in the Pacific, are simultaneously performances for simple and mass audiences, as were most of politicians' public appearances in the British general election of 1997.

With the advent of mass audiences, the notion of performance is altered. First, the performer has had to moderate his or her performance. For example, the characteristics that make for good political oratory in front of a simple audience do not necessarily play well for television. Orators find difficulty in being succinct on television and the tension that is so necessary when making a speech to a live audience can come across on television as nerves or even shiftiness. As Atkinson (1984) says:

> Practices which are visible, audible and impressive to those sitting in the back row of an auditorium or debating chamber are therefore likely to seem grossly exaggerated, unnatural and even oppressive when viewed on the small screen from a distance of a few feet A booming voice, poetic phrases, finely co-ordinated intonational cadences and expansive non-verbal actions are unlikely to impress when viewed at close quarters. (p. 176)

Similarly, acting styles which are suited to the theatrical stage do not necessarily fit in with the conventions of cinema. Naremore (1988), for example, notes a contrast between presentational and representational modes of acting. In the latter, chiefly used in the cinema, the performers are almost invisible, allowing a direct connexion between audience and character. At the same time the illusion is created that the audience is not present with the actors when they are performing. Presentational styles, on the other hand, recognize that the audience and the performers are in each other's presence and involve quite different conventions.

Second, the performance in a larger sense has also to be transformed in the movement from simple to mass audiences. In the early part of the twentieth century, mass media forms borrowed the conventions of performance in front of simple audiences. Film, for example, traded on the conventions of theatrical performance and was given its *authenticity* by a borrowing from live performance. The film was shot in long takes which largely followed the actual sequence of the finished product. By the 1930s, however, scenes from different parts of the film would be shot together and the whole created at the editing stage. Actors are only performing fragments and are not responsible for a complete piece, and this discontinuity implies that a movie performance is *built* not *shot*. Furthermore, the representation of a character may not be the work of a single actor. Stuntmen may carry out dangerous parts of the role, voices may be dubbed, and secondary actors may provide body parts, hands for example, at various times in the narrative. An extreme example is Hitchcock's *Psycho*, in which the performance of Mrs Bates is actually constructed out of the separate performances of three actors with three more providing voices (Maltby and Craven, 1995).

The history of recorded music follows a similar pattern. As Eisenberg (1988) says:

> The word 'record' is misleading. Only live recordings record an event; studio recordings, which are in the great majority, record nothing. Pieced together from bits of actual events, they construct an ideal event. They are like the composite photograph of a minotaur. Yet Edison chose the word deliberately. He meant his invention to record grandparents' voices, business transactions, and, as a last resort, musical performances. The use we put it to now might strike him as fraudulent, like doctoring the records. (p. 89)

This process of construction of a 'finished' product from a number of different components is made more complex with the advent of computer technologies. Andrew Goodwin (1992) identifies three key new technologies: the sequencer, the digital sampling music computer (the sampler) and MIDI (Musical Instrument Digital Interface). Sequencers automate the process of music making, allowing drum patterns, keyboard bass-lines, arpeggios, melodies, and so forth to be entered in 'real time' (a musician actually hits pads, electronic drum surfaces, or a synthesizer keyboard) in which the music is entered simply as information (with values such as the quarter note, for instance, or perhaps numerically constituted). The music can then be played back by the machine. It can also be manipulated by changing tempo, accuracy ('quantizing'), sequence, and sometimes timbre. (Goodwin, 1992, p. 78)

A sampler, as its name suggests, is used to 'sample' sounds which can then be altered in any number of different ways. MIDI allows the interconnexion of different machines so that they can interact. It is clear that mass audiences are responding to a constructed event on a different level in this respect.

The evolution of mass production techniques out of simple audience performances is not just a question of the process of performance *per se*. Audiences have also evolved along the same lines. In the early history of particular mass media, therefore, audiences treated the medium as if it were a simple performance. For example, earlier experiences of the cinema were modelled on the theatre. The design of the space, the ceremonies of attendance and the use of organ music all traded on the theatrical experience. Similarly in television, audiences were inclined to act as simple audiences. The curtains would be closed, the family would sit in a circle paying rapt attention, and no disturbances would be tolerated. In some cases, the stage of technological development meant that the simple performance was only available to a single-member audience at any one time. Thus, in the case of radio the early audience tended to be made up of enthusiasts who assembled their receivers from parts and listened to the signal over a set of headphones. However, radios were rapidly developed which both fitted with the decor of the domestic spaces in which they were located, and could be listened to by all members of the household at the same time (Moores, 1993; Scannell and Cardiff, 1991). This audience was also addressed in such a way as to reinforce this pattern in that the programmes were domestically orientated and broadcast live (Frith, 1983). These techniques and modes of address were then transferred to television where simple performances and established formats were adapted for the new medium. Spigel (1992), in her examination of the early days of television in the USA, points to the way in which established patterns of live entertainment and radio led to the pre-eminence of the 'family comedy', where, in 'a strange mix of naturalism and theatricality, the family comedy was a virtual "theatre of the everyday" that presented reality in a heightened, exaggerated fashion' (p. 159).

The processes involved in the creation of the mass media effectively greatly alter (but do not entirely transform) the notion of performance. In a culture dominated by the mass media, performances are *elongated* in time and space and *fragmented*. Perhaps even more fundamentally, a different *aesthetic* of performance comes into play.

So performances form an elongated chain or, as Thompson (1995) notes, there is a substantial degree of *time–space distanciation*. They travel over greater distance. Performances from the past, captured in some recording medium, can be replayed in the present. At the same time, performance is not spatially restricted but can be received well away from the context of the original event. As a result, it becomes less clear what set of processes constitute *the* performance, which is stretched out, for example, from the recording studio at one end to the playing of a record in the home, which is itself a performance of a kind, if a secondary one, at the other.

At the same time, performances to mass audiences are more fragmented, have a higher division of labour, than those to simple audiences. Of course, theatrical performances, or political meetings, are *productions* which involve a fairly large number of people in a detailed division of labour. Despite this, the actual performers are more central, take more of the responsibility, for the performance than they do in mass media events. The production of film, television or recorded music, for example, is spread over a large number of people, each of whom has a specialized function for which he or she has developed particular skills refined over often long periods of training and experience. In the modern mass media industries, the high division of labour, together with production techniques no longer dependent on the live performance, have given particular prominence to non-performers of a particular kind. Film producers and directors, television and record producers, make out of a set of raw and fragmented performances a complete whole.

Transformations in the mode of production of cultural objects imply that, in appreciating a mass media performance, audiences have to get used to a different aesthetic from the one that they might employ in attending a live performance. This is a *constructed aesthetic* rather than an *immediate aesthetic*. This means that aesthetic pleasure for a mass audience is no longer authorial, deriving from the individual voice of an immediately present person who is named and recognized. It instead derives from unseen heads and hands who, usually unrecognized, piece together a whole from fragments. This piecing together becomes an apparently technical exercise which gives a crucial role to such occupations as sound engineers and video editors, who, in displaying a 'sort of studio creativity', manifest the 'concept of the composer as engineer' (Frith, 1992, p. 44). We say 'apparently technical' because it is not merely technical. Actually video editing, for example, is as creative a function as the original direction of the video, and often more so. It is therefore entirely appropriate to refer to mass media forms as manifesting a constructed *aesthetic*. For this aesthetic, the live performance is no longer the ideal form; a mass media performance simply offers a different *kind* of experience that is equally valid aesthetically.

We have argued that simple performances are immediate – performer and audience are physically present at the same time. Mass media performances, on the other hand, are *mediated*. As McQuail (1987) points out, this can mean a variety of things. The media may lie between us and realms of experience with which we cannot have direct contact; they interpose between us and institutions like the state or the law; they provide channels of contact; and they give information which allows us to form opinions of other people, nations or events. There may also be a number of ways in which the mediation is carried out, 'varying especially in terms of degree and kind of activity, purposefulness, interactivity and effectiveness', and 'ranging from the direct relationship of one to another, through negotiations, to control of one by another' (p. 52). So, the mediation exercised by the institutions of the mass media between individuals and the outside world can take the form of a window, an interpreter, a platform, an interactive link, a signpost, a filter, a mirror or a screen or barrier.

Thompson (1995), more usefully, construes the notion of mediation in rather a different way as to do with the construction of different types of social interaction:

> we can understand the social impact of the development of new networks of communication and information flow only if we put aside the intuitively plausible idea that communication media serve to transmit information and symbolic content to individuals whose relations to others remain fundamentally unchanged. We must see, instead, that the use of communication media involves the creation of new forms of action and interaction in the social world, new kinds of social relationship and new ways of relating to others and to oneself. When individuals use communication media, they enter into forms of interaction which differ in certain respects from the type of face-to-face interaction which characterizes most encounters of daily life. They are able to act for others who are physically absent, or act in response to others who are situated in distant locales. (p. 4)

Thompson distinguishes three types of social interaction: face-to-face interaction, mediated interaction and mediated quasi-interaction. Face-to-face interaction generally demands the co-presence of the parties, it generally involves a two-way flow of communication, and messages are usually conveyed using a multiplicity of symbolic cues. Mediated interaction, on the other hand, uses some technical medium (telephone wires, paper, for instance) which allows communication without co-presence. The result is that mediated interaction is 'stretched across space and time'. It also involves a reduction in the range of symbolic cues; participants in the interaction can no longer depend on body language, for example, to help in the flow of communication. The advent of the mass media ushers in the possibility of mediated quasi-interaction, which is also stretched over space and time and also restricts the range of symbolic cues, but differs from both the other forms of interaction in that it is orientated no longer to specific others but to a potential indefinite number of participants; furthermore it is, generally speaking, a one-way traffic.

While simple audiences are physically and socially separated from the performers, it is obvious that the mass media of communication enforce even greater separation. We have already referred to the way in which mass audiences are spatially and temporally distanced from the original performance, such as it is. What is perhaps less obvious is that the *social* distance between performer and audience is also more pronounced. At a very simple level the social distance between star and audience is promoted by the difference in lifestyle. Stars frequently engage in conspicuous consumption. They are fashionably dressed, live in large houses, travel the world on expensive holidays and consort with the wealthy and aristocratic. Gossip and scandal go with the remoteness generated by wealth and lifestyle.

Social distance is represented in the acquisition by the star of an aura or a charismatic quality (see Dyer 1979, 1991). The star is set apart, extraordinary, endowed with special, almost superhuman, qualities. Such a quality simultaneously produces a sense of removal *and* a pervasive *interest* in the star's every action. It is rather more complex than this of course for there are actually different relationships between star and audience within the general framework of social distance. Tudor (1974), for instance, distinguishes four modes of star–audience relationship. Emotional affinity describes the state in which the audience member feels a loose attachment to the star. In a second mode, the audience member identifies so powerfully with the star that he or she actively places him- or herself in the position of the star. Third, the audience member imitates the star, adopting the clothes, hairstyle, language or walk. Fourth, this imitation can merge with projection, in which the audience member almost merges with the star and lives his or her life bound up with the star (see also Stacey, 1994).

Any identification between star and audience may, to some extent, seem to undermine the social distance between the two. The notion of identification seems to imply that members of the audience, in imagination, want to fuse identities with that of the star. It is important, however, to stress here how imagination works in this process (and we will return to the topic later in the book). Identification-in-imagination only works through difference and distance. As Stacey (1991) points out in her study of women's relationship to film stars based on letters describing their feelings towards such stars, many forms of identification depend either on worship at a distance or on a recognition of the gulf:

> the relationship between star and audience is also articulated through the recognition of an immutable difference between star and spectator: 'Bette Davis was the epitome of what we would like to be, but knew we never could!' (N. T). Yet here the desire to move across that difference and become more like the star is expressed, even if this is accompanied by the impossibility of its fulfilment. The distance between the spectator and her ideal seems to produce a kind of longing which offers fantasies of transformed identities. (p. 150)

Simple audiences attend in localized spaces. Mass audiences attend in global spaces. However, one should be wary here. In one sense mass audiences are global, but in another they are local. We have already pointed out that mass performances are elongated. This makes it difficult to say when a performance has taken place. There is the original performance, which is often recorded and is replayed in what is another performance, though of a different kind. This second performance frequently takes place in a private setting, local not global.

The privatization of reception is indeed an important feature of mass audiences. It is notable that performances for simple audiences are almost invariably in public spaces, whether they are plays, political meetings, public ceremonies or religious worship. It is arguable that the early history of the mass media was also played out in this public sphere, and some forms, cinema, for instance, still are. Public performance of this kind is also, in an important sense, *social*. People attend public performances at least partly for the sense of a relationship with other people in the audience. In appearing in a play or at a political meeting, performers are trading not only on a direct relationship *between* themselves and each audience member, but also on the relationships *between* audience members. When new forms of mass communication first appear, their reception is often social. For example, when television sets were first introduced, whole neighbourhoods would gather round. In communities in the third world where sets are less common, they are often treated as a public resource. Once established, however, the reception of mass communications is clearly private and domestic.

In an earlier section we argued that simple audience performances are accompanied by a great deal of ceremony and ritual which makes those performances extra-mundane. Indeed, the characteristic public space location of performances to simple audiences contributes to the sense of ritual. Clearly, the domestication and privatization of mass media audiences do deprive performances of this ritualistic quality. Since they are interwoven with the practices of everyday life in the home, they are literally mundane. However, it would be misleading to argue that there was no element of ritual for mass audiences. At times even the domestic reception of forms of the mass media can be ritualistic. Elements of ceremony attach to reading the newspaper in the morning or even watching television. Eisenberg (1988) formulates an even stronger argument for the act of listening to recorded music. He suggests that this is often accompanied by ritualistic activity as people deliberately sit down to listen to music. They sit comfortably, they fetch themselves a drink, they eliminate all distractions:

> The physical act of playing a record can itself be ritualistic. My own ancient AR turntable needs to be spun a few times by hand before the pulley and gears will catch, and the tone arm has to be lowered preliminarily beneath the level of the platter to get the damping right. No one else knows to do these things. My Levitical knowledge makes me master of all phonographic rites conducted in my home. But even modern machines want a good deal of attention to their levers and knobs. In fact, the more state-of-the-art the machine, the more attention it wants. (p. 43)

The connexion between ritual and the lack of distraction that Eisenberg identifies is revealing. In the discussion of simple audiences we argued that there was a relationship between ceremony and attention – the greater the ceremonial quality, the greater the attention given. For mass audiences, by contrast, the *relative* absence of ceremony in domestic spaces is related to low attention. Audiences for television, recorded music and magazines are essentially *distracted*, their attention half given to what else is going on around them; these media become background for everyday life. Contrast this with the powerful intensity with which audiences (for most of the time) attend to a play in circumstances where everything conduces to such attention.

While it makes sense to refer to mass audiences as low attention by comparison with simple audiences, it also over-simplifies. It would be more accurate to say that mass audiences move in and out of attention. For example, many households will have the television set on for most of the evening but pay particular attention to favourite programmes, soap opera for example. At the smaller scale, especially dramatic moments within any one pro-gramme may command audience attention which is then more easily distracted in periods of lessened tension (Abercrombie, 1996). This is even more the case with other media which are consumed in households. Popular music is often part of the fabric of domestic activity, either sourced from a radio or CD/tape player. An indication of the ways in which audience members can move in and out of attention can be found in the ways in which the lyrics of songs can be misheard. Parts of lyrics are heard correctly but others are interpreted to make sense to the listener without necessarily conforming to what the writer intended. Many writers see this variable attention as a consequence of the medium itself. Alloway (1992), for instance, claims that the

> repetitive and overlapping structure of modern entertainment works in two ways: (1) it permits marginal attention to suffice for those spectators who like to talk, neck, parade; (2) it satisfies, for the absorbed spectator, the desire for intense participation which leads to a careful discrimination of nuances in the action. (p. 702)

DIFFUSED AUDIENCES

Further fundamental social and cultural changes have produced a very different type of audience-experience, which we will call the *diffused audience*. The essential feature of this audience-experience is that, in contemporary society, everyone becomes an audience all the time. Being a member of an audience is no longer an excep-tional event, nor even an everyday event. Rather it is constitutive of everyday life. This is not a claim that simple audiences or mass audiences no longer exist. Quite the contrary. These experiences are as common as ever, but they take place against the background of the diffused audience. Indeed, as we shall show later, the three audience forms can feed off one another.

The notion of the diffused audience refers to several processes operating at different levels. First, people spend a lot of *time* in consumption of mass media in the home – and in public. This is a media-drenched society. Thus Gershuny and Jones (1987), in an investigation of a number of time-budget studies, concluded that, in the early 1980s, employed men were spending 158 minutes and employed women 122 minutes in the consumption of mass media of various kinds in every day.

If households are simply spending more time in the consumption of the mass media, a second and more fundamental argument is that the media are actually *constitutive* of everyday life. The media and everyday life have become so closely interwoven that they are almost inseparable. This is not just that the mass media are essentially private and directed at domestic life, the argument addressed earlier in the chapter. It is a claim that the very constitution and regulation of the mundane is in the hands of the media. An illustration of this can be taken from an interview study of the meaning of music in everyday life (Crafts et al., 1993, p. 109).

Q: What does music mean to you?
A: Music is just part of life, like air. You live with it all the time, so it's tough to judge what it means to you. For some people, it's a deep emotional thing, for some people, it's casual. I turn on the radio and it's there in the morning; it's there when I drive; it's there when I go out.
Q: If it isn't there, do you miss it?
A: No.
Q: So you're not really aware that it is there?
A: It's like a companion, or a back-up noise. Just something in the background. A lot of people turn the radio on and they're not listening to it for the most part, but it's there to keep them company, it's background noise. It's like the TV; they leave the TV on all the time, although it never gets watched. But it's background, people use it just to feel comfortable with.

Television has, relatively quickly in Western societies, become integrated into the routines of everyday life. Silverstone (1994) has formulated an account of the place of television in modern social life in which this everyday quality of the medium is central. He argues that our sense of security is maintained by the familiar routines of daily life, by our commonsense understandings and practical knowledge. An important part of this consists of rituals and symbols of which we may be largely unaware; 'The symbols of daily life: the everyday sights and sounds of natural language and familiar culture; the publicly broadcast media; text on billboards, in newspapers, on television; the highly charged and intense private and public rituals in domestic or national rites of passage or international celebrations' (Silverstone, 1994, p. 19). In this symbolic and ritualistic construction of everyday life, television has a crucial part to play, as an object in the room providing a focus for conversation, as a medium locating us in local, national and global relationships, and as an entertainer and informer.

One of the major ways in which everyday life is organized is by *time*. A sense of security is given by the routines that occur at more or less fixed times – going to bed, getting up, meal-times. Television has a major part to play in this fixing of events in time. Hobson (1982), for example, shows how her respondents integrated the now defunct soap opera *Crossroads* into their domestic lives. Viewers of the programme frequently referred to their viewing as a 'habit'. They did not mean anything negative in their use of this word but only that 'the regular scheduling of programmes which are transmitted at the same time means that those programmes become part of a certain "time band" in peoples' lives' (p. 115). A routine or habit develops in which *Crossroads* is integrated with tea-time or children's bed-time. The domestic and the televisual revolve around each other. So programming schedules are determined by the domestic pattern of life. The reverse is also true: household rhythms are organized around television programmes which can regulate meal-times, bed-times and occasions for going out.

A third way in which the diffused audience is created is via what Kershaw (1994) calls 'the performative society'. In this sense, performance has to be distinguished from theatre. As Roach (1995) puts it:

> Derived from the Greek word for seeing and sight, theater . . . is a limiting term for a certain kind of spectatorial participation in a certain kind of event. Performance, by contrast, though it frequently makes reference to theatricality as the most fecund metaphor for the social dimensions of cultural production, embraces a much wider range of human behaviors. (p. 46)

Kershaw (1996) notes the pervasiveness of performance in contemporary society:

> Simultaneously, the mediatisation of developed societies disperses the theatrical by inserting performance into everyday life – every time we switch into the media we are immediately confronted by a performative world of representational styles – and in the process the ideological functions of performance become ever more diverse and, maybe, diluted. Moreover, the globalisation of communications stages the life of other cultures as unavoidably performative, as widening realms of human identity become object to the spectators' gaze, and the social and political resonances of particular crises, such as the suffering of starving Somalians or the quasi-invasion of Haiti by the United States, are absorbed by the relentless opacity of the spectacle. (p. 133)

The performative society 'in which human transactions are complexly structured through the growing use of performative modes and frames' (Kershaw, 1994, p. 167), appears in almost every sphere of human activity in Western developed societies:

> in the development of the heritage and tourist industries, where costume drama – whether in the form of retro-dressing or the contemporary couture of slick uniforms – is increasingly the norm. It can be detected as easily in the associated industries of catering and travel, where the waiter and the air-host are encouraged to add a flick of performative spice to the fare. It appears in the retail industries, where the name tag on the check-out person confers an identity which has little to do with individual character, everything to do with a quasi-personalized and dramatized conception of service. (Kershaw, 1994, p. 166)

Or, it might be said, performance intrudes into even more mundane activities, the creation of 'everyday' shrines at accident sites,

especially road accidents, for example, or the tendency to pro-
claim birthdays with signs on the outsides of houses.

One of the effects of the intrusion of the media into everyday
life is the way that formerly innocent events become turned into
performances with the further result that the people involved in
those events come to see themselves as performers. For example,
the protests in Britain in the early 1990s in port towns against the
export of live animals will have started as a simple wish to stop
this trade. In a sense it was a simple performance which rapidly
becomes a performance for the mass media, as press and television begin to take an interest. At that point, the protesters see
themselves not only as making a moral and political point, but
also as performers for a variety of audiences. We return to this
point in more detail in Chapters 3 and 4.

In a rather different, and narrower, context the performative
society can be seen in an increasing tendency to see all art as
performance, whether it is sculpture, painting, music or drama
proper. Added to this is a parallel tendency to regard apparently
unartistic events of various kinds as performance *art*. Bernstein
(1977), for example, argues that the activities of the apparently
political guerrilla group the Symbionese Liberation Army in the
late 1960s and early 1970s should be treated as acts of performance
with decidedly artistic intentions and effects.

In the model of the performative society it is still possible to see
performances as discrete events. It is possible to identify and label
them *as* performances. This conception is put well by Schechner
(1993), who argues, familiarly, that the 'broad spectrum of performance' includes a whole variety of activity in a whole variety
of fields, all 'performative behaviour'. However, at the same time,
he suggests that all these behaviours can be seen in terms of
'various and complex relationships among players – spectators,
performers, authors, and directors – [which] can be pictured as a
rectangle, a performance quadrilogue' (p. 21). This conception of
performance, and of the performative society, we would argue,
still depends on a notion of performance as a discrete event.
However, at a still more fundamental level the diffused audience
experience may be characterized by the virtual *invisibility* of
performance – the fourth sense of the diffused audience. So

deeply infused into everyday life is performance that we are unaware of it in ourselves or in others. Life is a constant performance; we are audience and performer at the same time; everybody is an audience all the time. Performance is not a discrete event.

Of course, the argument that everyday life is a performance is a familiar one (for examples of various positions, see Carlson, 1996; Chaney, 1993; Sennett, 1977; Shevstova, 1989). As Simmel (1898) notes:

> In the same sense . . . in which we are poets and painters, we are also play actors; i.e. culture endows every aspect of life with this characteristic. Without being in any sense false or hypocritical, the personal existence of the individual is metamorphosed into some predetermined guise which is of course produced out of the resources of his own life, but is nevertheless not merely the straightforward expression of his own life. The possibility exists for us to assume such appearances, even strange ones, and nevertheless remain consistent with our own nature. (pp. 309–10)

Gurvitch (1955) similarly points to the theatricality implicit in the frequent ceremonial occurrences of everyday life, whether they be a hearing by a tribunal, a parliamentary session, a funeral, or the way in which even a 'simple reception or a sociable gathering contains explicit or implicit ceremonies' (p. 72). More systematically still, Gurvitch argues that the very notion of playing a role, fundamental to all social conduct, implies that all social life is performance. Human society itself is theatre. As Sennett (1977) points out, this conception has a long history from Plato and Petronius to Balzac, Mann and Baudelaire. For Sennett, until comparatively recently (actually until sociologists got their hands on the idea), the notion of society as theatre served three 'constant moral purposes'. First, illusion and delusion become intrinsic issues in social life; within the time and space of a particular social performance an illusion is created in which audiences can believe but outside it the illusion is difficult to sustain. Second, human nature becomes detached from social action. Since every man and woman is playing a different role in different social circumstances, one cannot read off their essential human natures from any one example of social action, any one performance. Third, 'the images of *theatrum mundi* are pictures of the art people exercise in ordinary life' (p. 35). There is, in everyday life, an *art* of acting.

A good deal of twentieth-century sociology, in that it makes extensive use of the concept of 'role', puts performance at the centre of the analysis of social behaviour. More recently, not only in sociology but also in performance theory, the notion that social life is performance has been most closely associated with the work of Goffman (see especially 1969 and 1974). From one point of view, the whole of Goffman's work is dedicated to an analysis of the rules, strategies and tactics of social interaction. Goffman employs stage analogies routinely in this analysis, especially in his *The Presentation of Self in Everyday Life* (1969). This is, in effect, to treat everyday interaction as performances, and Goffman defines performance as 'all activity of an individual which occurs during a period marked by his continuous presence before a particular set of observers and which has some influence on the observers' (p. 19). Such a very general definition indicates that performance is entirely pervasive in everyday life, and practically constitutive of it, and, indeed, makes it difficult to separate performance from non-performance.

In the fourth sense of the diffused audience, we diverge from these accounts of role-playing or social-life-as-theatre in two important respects. First, it is *specific* to contemporary society rather than being characteristic of human society in *general*. The notion of performance-in-everyday-life that we wish to employ suggests that such performances are more widespread in twentieth-century society than in earlier societies. It may well be true that social action in any society can best be described by the notion of role, but there is something peculiar to modern societies that gives the performances involved a particular twist. Indeed, this point is implicit in those writers who criticize Goffman for the absence of a sense of history in his work. Second, one of the reasons that modern societies are more performative is that the media of mass communications provide an important resource for everyday performance.

Much of the rest of this book (especially Chapters 3 and 4) is dedicated to an exploration of the way in which this sense of the diffused audience is modern. In brief, the diffused audience arises from the interaction of two processes, both of which are modern. On the one hand, there is the construction of the world as spectacle and, on the other, the construction of individuals as narcissistic. People simultaneously feel members of an audience and that they are performers; they are simultaneously watchers and being watched. As Rubin (1970) puts it in talking about street political action: 'Life is theatre and we are the guerrillas attacking the shrines of authority. . . . The street is the stage. You are the star of the show and everything you were once taught is up for grabs' (p. 250, quoted in Schechner, 1993, p. 64). Spectacle and narcissism feed off each other in a virtuous cycle, a cycle fuelled largely by the media and mediated by the critical role of performance. As with the other types of audience, performance is the key, but, unlike the other types, performance is not so linked to events, but has, so to speak, *leaked out* into the conduct of everyday life.

In terms of the characteristics described in Figure 2.1, the diffused audience is clearly a very different animal from both simple and mass audiences. A crucial feature is that the distance between performers and audiences so important to performances in front of both simple and mass audiences has been more or less eliminated. Rubin (1970) puts this brutally in an essay on 'Revolution is Theatre-in-the-Streets': 'You are the stage. You are the actor. Everything is for real. There is no audience' (p. 132, quoted in Schechner, 1993, p. 91). Since people are simultaneously performers and audience members, cultural consumers become cultural producers and vice versa. Being a member of a diffused audience is not necessarily to be in the position of receiving a message from a producer of messages; it is not like being *addressed* by a producer. We will argue later (in Chapters 5 and 6) that this homogenization of producers and consumers is related to the acquisition by audiences of *skills* of various kinds, the absence of which previously emphasized the distance between performers and audience. In the right circumstances, audience members use these skills to become cultural producers in their own right inside what we shall call *enthusiasms*.

As far as the other features described in Figure 2.1 are concerned, communication is direct and unmediated; media institutions do not interpose between performer and audience. There is little or no ceremony for these are the practices of everyday life. Attention is generally low or variable, switching from intense concentration to relative inattention. Diffused audiences are both local and global, local in actual performance, global in that imagination – not restricted in space and time – is a crucial resource in the performance. Performances for diffused audiences are public *and* private. Indeed, they erode the difference between the two.

The potential for erosion of the distinction between private and public inherent in diffused audiences performances suggests a general characteristic of this audience form – the breaking of boundaries. Specifically, we would argue that performance events, or media events, cannot be distinguished so well from one another and, indeed, there is a fusion of different *forms* of the media.

This issue of boundaries clearly relates to claims made about postmodernism and postmodernist art. Rothenberg (1977), for example, argues that there is 'an unquestionable and far-reaching breakdown of boundaries and genres; between "art and life" (Cage and Kaprow), between various conventionally defined arts (intermedia and performance art), and between arts and non-arts (musique concrète, found art, etc.)' (p. 13). For example:

> – that there is a continuum, rather than a barrier, between music and noise; between poetry and prose (the language of inspiration and the language of common and special discourse); between dance and normal locomotion (walking, running, jumping), etc.
> – that there is no hierarchy of media in the visual arts, no hierarchy of instrumentation in music, and that qualitative distinctions between high and low genres and modes (opera and vaudeville, high rhetoric and slang) are no longer operational. (p. 13)

3

Spectacle and Narcissism

In Chapter 2 we distinguished four levels at which one could speak of the diffused audience. First, people spend a lot of *time* in the consumption of mass media. For example, as Lewis (1991) notes, whereas earlier in the century most people spent their time working and sleeping, from 1950 or so they work, sleep and watch television. Second, the media are intensely pervasive in that they are very difficult to avoid in everyday life. Indeed, the media and everyday life have become so closely interwoven that they are almost inseparable. Third, contemporary society is a performative society. A good deal of human activity is constructed as a performance, whether it concerns the airline stewardesses' greeting of passengers embarking on the aircraft or the complex interactions involved in touring a stately home. Fourth, and most fundamental, diffused audiences are the result of the interaction of two processes, spectacle and narcissism. At all of these four levels it is clear that the omnipresence of the media, the increasing development of media skills, and the way in which the media function as a resource for everyday life are critical to the formation of the diffused audience, and, as we argued in Chapter 2, it is this that distinguishes the idea of the diffused audience from the more general notion of social life as drama. The diffused audience, in other words, is *modern*.

The four levels at which one can understand the concept of the diffused audience are all related to one another, in particular by the pervasiveness of the media. While the bulk of this chapter concentrates on the fourth level, we will necessarily discuss the other three.

SPECTACLE

In arguing for the importance of spectacle, the proposition is that the world, and everything in it, is increasingly treated as *something to be attended to* (Chaney, 1993). The people, objects and events in the world cannot simply be taken for granted but have to be framed, looked at, gazed upon, registered and controlled. In turn, this suggests that the world is constituted as an event, as a *performance*; the objects, events and people which constitute the world are made to perform for those watching or gazing.

This is clearly not an exclusively modern phenomenon. One familiar historical illustration lies in the literature on the history of the perception of landscape from the end of the seventeenth to the middle of the nineteenth centuries in Europe. The argument is that landscape as it has been *moulded*, *perceived* and *represented* is not some neutral object of nature but is instead a spectacle, performance or event. One way of putting this is to argue that landscape is discursively constructed. Green (1990), for example, shows the way in which nature was defined as countryside in nineteenth-century France. 'It has been argued that the "nature" of early nineteenth century France was an historically specific construct, a product of discourses materially grounded in the conditions of contemporary Paris' (p. 184). Pugh (1990) similarly argues that 'landscape and its representations are a "text" and are, as such, "readable" like any other cultural form' (p. 2).

During this period, many landscapes were deliberately *moulded* to *look* like pictures. From the fifteenth to the late seventeenth centuries English gardens were heavily influenced by Italian fashions and, to a lesser extent, by those drawn from French and Dutch examples (see, for example, Hadfield, 1985; Hyams, 1971). These influences produced gardens that were rigidly architectural and were designed 'formally, geometrically, anti-naturally, as settings for social activities' (Hyams, 1971, p. 3). By the early eighteenth century this style of gardening and landscaping was giving way to a more distinctively English set of practices. Gardens were to be conceived as *pictures of nature*. The landscape was thus artfully rearranged as if it were a picture. Although the intention was that the effect should look natural, in fact, of course, substantial feats of engineering were often involved. Capability Brown, for example, in creating his picturesque landscapes, moved hills, large trees and even whole villages. The landscaping was also based on a particular view of nature which involved an apparent superficial disorder but was in fact underpinned by a fundamental sense of order. Owing much to platonic idealism, this was not a reproduction of nature but rather an attempt to perfect and idealize it. 'So the garden artists set themselves, in making their gardens, to do what the landscape painters did in their pictures: to restore an entirely imaginary pristine perfection to nature – perfection, that is, in the sense that an artist might give the word' (Hyams, 1971, p. 9).

At the same time, landscapes were *perceived* as spectacles. This habit is clearly indicated in the invention of the Claude glass, an eighteenth-century device taken on carriage tours of the country-side. This was a blackened convex mirror which acted as a kind of picture frame that was held up to frame views of the countryside. Nature was not simply *there*, it had to be made an object of spectacle. In the same manner, Murdoch (1990) describes the activities of John Wilson, much influenced by the Picturesque movement, who, in the early nineteenth century, built a house in the Lake District 'of which the guiding architectural principle was to take advantage of the site and to use the house, as it were, *as a camera to take and present the views*' (p. 124, our emphasis).

Landscape was also *represented* as spectacle. The notion that nature became an object of spectacle in poetry, painting, literature and music is a well-trampled topic in writing on the Picturesque, Romantic and Gothic movements and we are not going to rehearse it extensively here. The point, clearly, is that not only did people begin to look upon landscape as a spectacle, as a series of performances, but they also demanded representations which enabled them to conceive of these spectacles in imagination. For example, Green (1990) notes the enormous popularity of nature painting in early nineteenth-century France:

> Topographical views, spectacular mountain scenery from Italy or the Pyrenees, cosy farmyard scenes with thatched cottages and cheery peasant girls, mysterious gothic ruins lit by moonlight; all these and more are regular items in any dealer's stock. At Giroux's 1830 auction of art stock, out of one hundred and twenty-five pieces, fifty-six can be classified by title as landscapes, sixteen as architectural views and several more as marines. (p. 98)

To see landscape as moulded, perceived and represented as spectacle is a specific example of the more general claim that the world is treated as composed of objects and events that are performing and therefore have to be attended to. For example, Urry (1990) understands modern tourism as a gaze encompassing spectacles of various kinds.

> The tourist gaze is directed to features of landscape and townscape which separate them off from everyday experience. Such aspects are viewed because they are taken to be in some sense out of the ordinary. . . . People linger over such a gaze which is then normally visually objectified or captured through photographs, postcards, films, models and so on. These enable the gaze to be endlessly reproduced and recaptured'. (p. 3)

When tourists travel they expect to treat the world as a series of spectacles – mountains, sunsets, folk-dances, stereotypical inhabitants, strange money, different food – all features to which they pay *attention*. As Urry points out, this attentiveness to spectacle is shown well in the taking of photographs, a practice entirely characteristic of modern tourism. By this means, tourists clearly treat their surroundings as a series of spectacles; objects and events perform through the camera lens. However, they also capture the images for later consideration and reflection. It goes without saying that the tourist industry goes to ever more ingenious lengths to manufacture more and more spectacular spectacles. For example, complex theme parks are developed in which large sums of money are invested. More revealingly still, the apparently mundane is transformed so that it becomes spectacular. Wigan becomes an attraction, areas of the Yorkshire Dales are christened 'Herriot country' or 'Brontë country', and Winchester Cathedral adds to its secular and religious uses a show of the

'Crusades experience'. In sum, as in the case of landscape discussed earlier, the tourist spectacle consists in the interaction of
the three moments: the moulding of tourist sites as spectacles, the
perception of those sites as spectacles by tourists, and the representation of tourist spectacles not only by means of photography,
but also by souvenirs, travel brochures, and so on. This account of
tourism, incidentally, shows the primacy of the sense of sight in
the construction of spectacle (Macnaghten and Urry, 1998), for the
metaphors used in the description of the spectacular experience
are almost invariably visual. Other senses may be employed in the
presentation and appropriation of spectacle but they are organized
by vision.

Although he starts his discussion of tourism as if it was an
extra-mundane set of experiences, Urry (1990) makes the important point that the boundary between tourism and everyday life
in modern (or postmodern) society has become fuzzy and per-
meable.

> What I have termed the tourist gaze is increasingly bound up with and
> is partly indistinguishable from all sorts of other social and cultural
> practices. This has the effect, as 'tourism' per se declines in specificity,
> of universalising the tourist gaze – people are much of the time
> 'tourists' whether they like it or not. The tourist gaze is intrinsically
> part of contemporary experience. . . . (p. 82)

Contemporary life in general is a question of spectacle and the
aim of modern life is to see and be seen, an aim that has come to
dominate leisure activities of all kinds and not just tourism but
also work and home life.

The question remains as to what extent the construction of the
world as spectacle is modern. There are two points to make. First,
there is simply the matter of degree: in contemporary society, the
world is more thoroughgoingly treated as an object of spectacle.
The spectacular gaze is no longer restricted to particular events,
occasions or objects but is instead a more pervasive feature of
everyday life. In a sense, the world becomes alive in a process of
reverse reification. This is not to assert a perverse sociological
animism but to recognize, amongst other things, the important
role of commodification in the creation of a spectacular society, a

topic to be taken up in a moment. The world-as-commodity demands attention; it performs (Appadurai, 1986; Kopytoff, 1986). In addition, the pervasiveness of the media of mass communication, as we shall argue later on, contributes to the presentation of the world as spectacle, as a set of performances. Landscape becomes mediascape.

Debord (1994), in his classic discussion of the spectacle, identifies a second feature which makes spectacular society modern. Contemporary society makes the world into spectacle because it is organized by capitalism, which has commodified everything and has thereby colonized everyday life. As Clark (1984) points out, this colonization 'points to a massive internal extension of the capitalist market – the invasion and restructuring of whole areas of free time, private life, leisure, and personal expression' (p. 9). Further:

> The concept of spectacle is thus an attempt – a partial and unfinished one – to bring into theoretical order a diverse set of symptoms which are normally treated, by bourgeois sociology or conventional Leftism, as anecdotal trappings affixed somewhat lightly to the old economic order: 'consumerism', for instance, or the 'society of leisure'; the rise of mass media, the expansion of advertising, the hypertrophy of official diversions (Olympic Games, party conventions, biennales). (p. 9)

Contemporary society is a consumer society. In looking at the world around them, people are increasingly therefore looking at commodities, objects or services that are produced for sale, marketed and sold. One might describe the gaze that is characteristic of modern society as a *possessive* gaze. This phrase is used by Berger (1972) in his discussion of oil painting in the period 1500–1900 in Europe and is defined as 'a way of seeing the world, which was ultimately determined by new attitudes to property and exchange' and which 'found its visual expression in the oil painting' (p. 87). What does this mean? Directly in Berger's text it means two things. First, pictures are themselves possessions. They can be bought and sold and hung on walls to indicate wealth and prestige. Much more important for Berger, however, they *depict* possessions. For example, various genres of oil painting involve the rendering of objects or scenes that can be owned – still lifes, *objets d'art*, farm animals. Landscapes, with their owners in the foreground, show off the ownership of rolling acres. The essential point is that this tradition in painting represents tangible substance – which is, technically, what oil painting is good at. A similar point can be made about landscape gardening. Page (1962), for example, argues that the English garden is deeply imbued with a sense of property. However, interestingly, this does not consist in emphasizing boundaries to property so that the owner, in surveying his or her garden, may there see what is literally and exclusively his or hers. To the contrary, boundaries are suppressed so that the garden gives a *limitless* sense of property.

> The English ideal is that no boundary should show. Even the line of demarcation between outdoors and indoors is obscured as far as possible by bringing planting up to and on to the walls of the house. In fact, the typical English garden, large or small, has for centuries been arranged so that, as far as possible, all that its owner can see shall appear as part of his garden (pp. 96–7)

This last sentence indicates a more subtle sense of the possessive gaze that might be implicit in Berger's work. In this sense, people gaze upon the world, as a world of spectacles, *as if* it were owned or could be potentially owned. It is not that the perceived world and its contents *is* owned or even that it realistically *could* be owned. It is that it is gazed upon by people who are owners in other respects and see everything in that light. The possessive gaze is grasping and internalizing. The contrast is with a gaze that is externalizing, that plays with the objects of spectacle, that rents not owns. In *this* sense of the possessive gaze that encompasses the world of spectacle, we depart somewhat from that considerable body of literature, largely influenced by the work of Foucault, that sees a spectacular society as involving a gaze of surveillance and control. Of course a gaze that involves ownership will also necessarily entail control. In our view, however, the ownership is primary and the control secondary. In essence, therefore, if one wants to understand how the spectacular society works, one has to understand how possession and ownership works, and that, in turn, must depend on an understanding of the workings of the capitalist mode of production.

To return to Debord (1994). The objects and events in the world, therefore, acquire a kind of life given by the possibility of ownership. They attract the fascinated gaze. In a sense they are *performing*. Debord himself, in a set of propositions that anticipate more recent debates, argues that

> The whole life of those societies in which modern conditions of production prevail presents itself as an immense accumulation of spectacles. All that was once directly lived has become mere representation. (p. 12)

While in earlier capitalist societies there was a transformation in human experience from 'being' to 'having', in late capitalist societies 'having' has become 'appearing'. The transformation of the world into an array of images is intimately related to the development of the commodity form:

> The spectacle corresponds to the historical moment at which the commodity completes its colonization of social life. It is not just that the relationship to commodities is now plain to see – commodities are now all that there is to see; the world we see is the world of the commodity. (p. 29)

Or, as Debord famously puts it, 'The spectacle is *capital* accumulated to the point where it becomes image' (p. 24). Debord also points out that the nature of the spectacular society becomes transformed as capitalism develops. Two stages of development are of particular significance. In its earlier phases the spectacle is *concentrated*. As the commodity form becomes even more widespread, the spectacle becomes *diffuse*. It is all around and fragmented, diffused throughout and infused into everyday life – just like the diffused audience.

It is important to note also that the spectacle which comprises external reality does not consist of inanimate objects. Just as the eighteenth-century Arcadian scene viewed from a country house would have consisted in a carefully landscaped park *and* both animals and people, so also is the modern spectacle a necessary fusion of inanimate and animate objects, all of which are *perform-*

ing in the spectacle. For example, Debord notes the importance of stars in the society of the spectacle.

> Media stars are spectacular representations of living human beings, distilling the essence of the spectacle's banality into images of possible roles. Stardom is a diversification in the semblance of life – the object of an identification with mere appearance which is intended to compensate for the crumbling of directly experienced diversifications of productive activity. (p. 38)

The process of spectacle is, in turn, closely related to another process said to be characteristic of modern (or postmodern) societies – the aestheticization of everyday life. This is again a well-trampled field and we summarize here the main interconnected themes that relate to our argument.

First, there is the claim that modern societies are dominated by *style*. A major preoccupation is with the appearance of things and their stylistic coherence with other things. This aesthetic concern is everywhere – and everyone. As Ewen (1988) says:

> Style was definitely more than a question of fashions in clothing or in literary expression. It was part of an ether, a general sensibility that touched on countless arenas of everyday life, yet was limited by none of them. It was something intangible yet important, everywhere and nowhere, inchoate. (p. 3)

Style is all about surfaces, a glittering array of surfaces. It lacks substance and can come and go in a trice. In contemporary societies it can be drawn from a bewildering variety of sources. 'The stylish person may look like a duchess one week, a murder victim the next. Style can hijack the visual idiom of astronauts, or poach from the ancient pageantry of Guatemalan peasant costume' (p. 14). If interest in style contributes to the aestheticization of everyday life, then so does *design*. In order to pander to a concern with style, commodities have to have a higher design component. When looking at an iron, a cooker or a car, people are considering the style aspects of the objects. Added value does not come, in other words, from greater functionality but from the aesthetic realm. Jameson (1991), for example, notes that capitalism's need to provide ever more novel-seeming goods, at ever greater rates of turnover, demands dedicated aesthetic innovation and experimentation. It is the design elements that not only give a competitive originality to commodities but also give them built-in obsolescence. At the same time capitalist production shifts from the production of goods to the production of services, or, as Harvey (1989) points out, to the production of events. These last have intrinsically a much higher design content. In addition, while culture represents a higher part of value in contemporary commodities, the culture industries themselves are becoming increasingly commodified. As their importance in giving added value increases, the writing of books, the composition of music, the creation of painting or sculpture, all become industries no different from any other.

As everyday life becomes more aestheticized, so also does art become more like everyday life. From this direction also art and everyday life come closer together. Thus Featherstone (1991) notes three senses in which artistic practice begins to take an interest in the mundane. First, the boundary between high and popular culture may be undermined by de-emphasizing the auratic quality of art. Art is no longer to be found exclusively in museums and galleries but can be discovered in the practices and culture of ordinary life, including what passes for popular culture. Second, and closely related, there is also the assumption that

> art can be anywhere or anything. The detritus of mass culture, the debased consumer commodities, could be art (here one thinks of Warhol and pop art). Art was also to be found in the anti-work: in the 'happening', the transitory 'lost' performance which cannot be museumified, as well as in the body and other sensory objects in the world. (p. 66).

Third, life can be turned into a work of art. Artists' lives themselves become the work of art. Featherstone notes that this has been a common feature of late nineteenth- and twentieth-century art. The notion is that through dress, opinions, furnishings, tastes and behaviour, the artist demonstrates a coherent and consistent aesthetic sensibility. The dandy is the forerunner of such a sensibility, manifesting in his person 'an uncompromising exemplary lifestyle in which the aristocracy of spirit manifested itself in a

contempt for the masses and the heroic concern with the achievement of originality and superiority in dress, demeanour, personal
habits' (p. 67).

The most important factor of all in the promotion of the
aestheticization of everyday life is the proliferation of *images*, or, as
Featherstone (1991) puts it, in 'the rapid flow of signs and images
which saturate the fabric of everyday life in contemporary society'
(p. 67). Baudrillard is the most commonly quoted source of this
idea. From a theory rooted in a semiological rendering of Marx's
account of commodities, he argues that images (signs) come to
have a life of their own independent of the objects of which they
are images. They become available for any use and hence the
consumer is bombarded with images deprived of their original
context. The machinery of image production – television, advertising, radio, music, newspapers, magazines – is so pervasive that
consumers begin to confuse image and reality, and, as Featherstone puts it, are taken 'beyond stable sense'. The proliferation of
images takes many and varied forms. For example, organizations
of all kinds adopt some icon by which they may be immediately
recognized; images become more important than text in advertisements; in much modern film the narrative is often much less
important than the visual spectacle (Lash, 1990). The notion of
image has, moreover, been extended beyond these visual examples. Harvey (1989), for example, notes the importance of 'image'
to politicians and 'brands' to companies. 'The production and
marketing of such images of permanence and power require
considerable sophistication, because the continuity and stability of
the image have to be retained while stressing the adaptability,
flexibility, and dynamism of whoever or whatever is being
imaged' (p. 288). What may be true of companies is also true of
the labour market. People are concerned to appear in the right
clothes, have the right car and go to image consultants to make
doubly sure that they appear to others as they would wish. All
these creations of image are intended to build up a distinctive
identity which gives, or maintains, a strong position in a competitive world.

In this proliferation of images the media play a crucial, if not *the*
crucial, part. As we have argued at several points in this book,

people in contemporary society spend a great deal of time surrounded by, or immersed in, images of various kinds, and the industries responsible for the production of these images grow in economic importance. Thompson (1990) puts it thus:

> Today we live in a world in which the extended circulation of symbolic forms plays a fundamental and ever-increasing role. In all societies the production and exchange of symbolic forms – of linguistic expressions, gestures, actions, works of art and so on – is, and has always been, a pervasive feature of social life. But with the advent of modern societies, propelled by the development of capitalism in early modern Europe, the nature and extent of the circulation of symbolic forms took on a new and qualitatively different appearance. Technical means were developed which, in conjunction with institutions oriented towards capital accumulation, enabled symbolic forms to be produced, reproduced and circulated on a hitherto unprecedented scale. . . . These developments in what is commonly called mass communications received a further impetus from advances in the electrical codification and transmission of symbolic forms, advances which have given us the varieties of electronic tele-communication characteristic of the twentieth century. (p. 1)

In sum, the aestheticization of everyday life encourages the widespread use of spectacle. It is the purpose, after all, of representation to draw the attention. The more the world becomes aestheticized, the more it becomes drenched in images, the more it becomes a cultural object, the more will it become something that invites being looked at. People, objects, events, *perform* for the diffused audience through their involvement in a richly symbolic world of spectacle.

NARCISSISM

We turn now to look at what is, from the point of view of the diffused audience, the other side of the coin of the spectacular society. Spectacle does not work to create the diffused audience without the simultaneous development of the narcissistic society.

The notion of a narcissistic society embodies the idea that people act as if they are being looked at, as if they are at the centre of the attention of a real or imaginary audience. It is important to note at the outset that we have in mind here a relatively restricted sense of the term 'narcissism' which nevertheless can adequately describe a way of behaving and thinking that is characteristic of a society as a whole and is not therefore restricted to a particular personality type. The idea, and the word, comes, of course, from the ancient Greek myth of Narcissus. Narcissus was an extraordinarily beautiful youth courted by suitors of both sexes. He spurned them all and one day sent the most insistent of them a sword. This suitor used the sword to kill himself on Narcissus' threshold, calling upon the gods to avenge him. They heard him and made Narcissus fall in love with himself. One day, while out hunting, he came to a pure stream and threw himself down to drink. There he saw an image of a beautiful boy with whom he instantly fell in love. After a while, he realized that he was looking at a reflection of himself, and his initial rapture turned to grief at the impossibility of possession. Eventually his grief overcame him and he killed himself. His blood soaked the earth and up sprang the white narcissus.

Elements of the myth of Narcissus have been used for different purposes, as we shall show in the following discussion. Everyday speech has taken from it the idea of self-love to apply to 'narcissists'. The psychoanalytical literature, in describing the narcissistic personality type, also focuses on self-love but adds to it the self-hate implicit in Narcissus' suicide. Also of interest to writers in the psychoanalytic tradition is the quality of unmet – and impossible – desire. Narcissus killed himself because he could not possess his love; contemporary narcissists are condemned to a lifetime of unfulfilled yearning. The account of narcissism that we want to employ to support the idea of the diffused audience draws on a different element of the myth. This is the image of the mirror implicit in Narcissus' falling in love with his *reflection*. It is as if the boundary between the external world and Narcissus is removed; when looking at the world all he sees is a reflection of himself. The importance of this element of the myth is reinforced by a less well-known aspect of the story. Narcissus' most persistent lover was the nymph Echo, who was only able to use her voice to repeat what others said. She was present at his death and hence echoed his last words: 'Ah, youth, beloved in vain, farewell!' (Graves,

1960). In doing this she reflected him reflecting himself – a hall of mirrors. An auditory reflection is added to a visual one. We now take up these points in more detail.

The recent discussion of the phenomenon of narcissism owes much to the work of Lasch (1980). For Lasch, narcissism describes a particular personality type characteristic of a fairly large number of people in Western societies but critically predominant in those who have risen to positions of influence. He adduces a catalogue of attributes of this personality type: a tendency to live in the present and to have no sense of the past or of the future; a dependence on others combined with a fear of such dependence; a worship of celebrity; an inner emptiness; a pseudo self-insight related to a dedicated interest in personal therapies of all kinds; nervous self-deprecatory humour; fiercely competitive yet fearful of competition; decline of the spirit of play; praising of teamwork yet harbouring deeply antisocial impulses; intensely acquisitive and demanding immediate gratification. Fundamental to all these traits, however, is the difficulty the narcissist experiences in distinguishing the boundaries of the self, in separating him- or herself from others. The narcissistic self is constructed and maintained only in the reflections received from others:

> Notwithstanding his occasional illusions of omnipotence, the narcissist depends on others to validate his self-esteem. He cannot live without an admiring audience. His apparent freedom from family ties and institutional constraints does not free him to stand alone or to glory in his individuality. On the contrary, it contributes to his insecurity, which he can overcome only by seeing his 'grandiose self' reflected in the attentions of others, or by attaching himself to those who radiate celebrity, power, and charisma. For the narcissist, the world is a mirror . . . . (p. 10)

The narcissistic society comes from any single cause but from 'bureaucracy, the proliferation of images, therapeutic ideologies, the rationalization of the inner life, the cult of consumption, and in the last analysis from changes in family life and from changing patterns of socialization' (p. 32). At work the narcissist is not interested in achieving anything but instead in seeming to be successful. In modern bureaucracies work takes on an almost abstract quality which is divorced from performance and thus encourages the narcissist. At the same time, modern life is thoroughly mediated by images of many kinds. Images come to be taken for reality and people come to see themselves as their images. Contemporary society is also dominated by the therapeutic sensibility, by an interest in health and fitness. As a result, people are constantly examining themselves for signs of illness, somatic or psychological. More fundamentally, however, the causes of the narcissistic personality lie in the child-rearing practices of modern society. For Lasch, the characteristic mode of child-rearing is a combination of intense concentration on the child without any real empathy. A great deal of attention is lavished but with shallow, perfunctory care. 'The combination of emotional detachment with attempts to convince a child of his favoured position in the family is a good prescription for a narcissistic personality structure' (p. 50). In turn, these features arise from family structure, which has turned in on itself and tries to defend itself from the pressures of a menacing world of business, jobs and politics by creating a façade of togetherness.

Sennett (1977) offers an account of narcissism that is similar in many respects to Lasch's. For him, narcissism is a character disorder that is normal or common in, or at least symptomatic of, modern societies. It makes sense, therefore, to speak of a narcissistic society. The condition consists fundamentally in an inability to distinguish the self from the world; the self in modern society is 'boundaryless'. It is 'a self-absorption which prevents one from understanding what belongs within the domain of the self and self-gratification and what belongs outside it' (p. 8). Curiously enough, this dedication to self-gratification also obstructs its fulfilment. Narcissism makes the person feel that, at the moment of gratification, this is not what he or she wants. A number of features result from this contradiction. The narcissist is unable to take in anything new since everything is seen in terms of the already-existing self. The narcissist feels empty since desire is never followed by true gratification. The narcissist is deprived of the ability to play. Indeed Sennett believes that narcissism and asceticism have much in common. 'In both, there is a projection of the self onto the world, rather than an engagement in worldly experience beyond one's control' (p. 334). For the narcissist, social transactions are all concerned with motivation, not with action or doing. 'The self no longer concerns man as actor or man as maker; it is a self composed of intentions and possibilities' (p. 263).

Narcissism is a psychic state potentially available in any society, but its development is encouraged by particular cultural formations. It is most especially encouraged by the growth of the intimate society, in which personal warmth and intimacy are the fundamental aims of life, aims which are realized (or not) in the private sphere of the family. More fundamentally still, the rise of secularism and capitalism contribute to the process because they both erode 'belief in experience external to the self. Together they have eroded the self as an aggressive, confident force, and instead made its very worthiness the object of obsessive anxiety' (p. 334).

How can these two accounts be related to the sense of narcissism that we wish to employ? First, both Lasch and Sennett delve into the psychoanalytical literature – often the same literature – for their conception of narcissism. Their image of narcissism is very much one of pathological deviation, a distortion of the self. Such a notion is indeed at the root of commonsense understandings of the personality type. For our purposes, however, narcissism should be seen more as a cultural condition, diffused widely, rather than a personality disorder. Second, as both Lasch and Sennett observe, narcissism should not be confused, as it so often is, with self-love. It is just as likely to be manifested as self-hate. From our point of view, however, the degree to which narcissism is associated with self-love or self-hate is not important. What *is* important is that the self is central and is central to an *audience* – a diffused audience – real or imagined. There is no boundary between the self and the world of people and things and so what stands outside the self is merely a reflection, as in a mirror, of the self (as in Narcissus' stream).

This point about the relationship between the self and an audience of others leads to a third consideration. Although the self is central, that does not mean that all else is obliterated. On the contrary, an *active* audience of other, and individual, selves is required, although it is an audience whose purpose is to reflect the central self. Indeed, for the proper functioning of narcissism, the audience has to be imagined as contributing to the narcissist's image of him- or herself. As Stacey (1994) notes: 'My argument is that narcissism is not just love of self, but always involves an image of the other' (p. 30). For 'other', Stacey has in mind ideal images such as film stars, but the argument can surely be extended.

A fourth point concerns the connexion between narcissism and *performance*. Our argument is that narcissism involves an imagined performance in front of others who constitute an audience which is focused on the narcissistic self. Lasch also takes the view that performance and narcissism are inextricably linked. He notes that within the performing arts, the gap between actors and audience is growing ever narrower, with the result that the audience is drawn more and more into performance. More widely, modern societies have a 'sense of the self as a performer under the constant scrutiny of friends and strangers' (p. 90), and 'in everyday life the average man became a connoisseur of his own performance and that of others' (p. 91). Sennett, it should be noted, does not take a similar view. In fact, he appears to argue the opposite, claiming that the performances that defined public life in eighteenth-century European cities are not compatible with a narcissistic society because acting is not possible in the intimate relationships that characterize such a society. However, his sense of performance is narrower than the one that we have employed in Chapter 2.

One way in which narcissism is linked necessarily with performance is via the importance of appearance and style. An adequate performance demands attention to the outward face, and the management of appearance is therefore a major preoccupation. Hence, a dedicated interest in clothes, perfume, hairstyle, home furnishing, cars, houses, music, food. It is the image as much as the substance of these issues of personal taste that matters. This connexion between narcissism and appearance is well put by a fashion model talking about her occupation: 'It's an addiction because you exist through others' eyes. When they stop looking at you, there's nothing left' (Rudolph, 1991, p. 75 quoted in Craik, 1994, p. 91). Narcissistic imaginings of being at the centre of attention because of the adoption of a certain style of appearance are essentially to do with what kind of person you are, with identity. For example, Craik (1994) notes that women's magazines are selling an 'ideal selfhood' by means of fashion articles and advertisements that give women an image not only to identify with, but also to clothe the body as the imagined centre of an audience; 'clothed bodies are tools of self-management' (p. 46). Or, as one of Ewen's (1988) respondents said:

> When I was in high school I cut out an advertisement from a magazine and hung it on my wall. The ad read 'Create An Image' in big bold white letters. . . . I don't remember what the ad was for, and I never really cared. . . . I simply wanted to remind myself to work on my style. . . . I used to be really taken by someone who could cause that intense silence just by entering a room. I was often captured by their style. (p. 20)

Narcissism cannot be treated as an isolated phenomenon. As an aspect of modernity it is closely connected with what has been called the 'project of the self'. Both Lasch and Sennett hold to a view of this sort, as we have already noted. The former, for example, sees narcissism as related to a modern quest for personal therapies of all sorts in which the security, maintenance and development of the self is seen as an all-important life aim. Sennett (1977) sees narcissism as encouraged by 'the intimate society' which sees authentic relationships between individuals, in which the most intimate depths of personality are plumbed, as the ultimate good: 'social relationships of all kinds are real, believable, and authentic the closer they approach the inner psychological concerns of each person' (p. 259).

The project of the self is a rather more general category than narcissism, which refers to a specific set of personality characteristics. It can be represented in a wide range of modern behaviours. For example, Heelas (1992, 1994, 1996) argues that a great deal of contemporary spiritual experience, especially New Age religious experience, is founded in 'the turn to the self' or 'self-spirituality'. New Age beliefs, which in one way or another are held by a large number of people, emphasize 'self-development', 'self-actualization', 'getting in touch with feelings' and 'being oneself'.

'The key belief of those who are at the heart of the "New Age", namely self-religionists, is that nothing less than God lies within' (Heelas, 1992, p. 139).

In much influential recent social theory the essence of the project of the self lies in the idea of reflexivity (Beck, 1992; Giddens, 1990, 1991, 1992; Lash and Urry, 1994). Giddens, for example, holds that reflexivity is a condition of modernity. In a sense, reflexivity is a defining characteristic of human action in every society. In modernity, however, it takes on a particular character. 'The reflexivity of modern social life consists in the fact that social practices are constantly examined and reformed in the light of incoming information about those very practices, thus constitutively altering their character' (Giddens, 1990, p. 38). In this context, one of the key features of modernity is what Giddens calls 'the reflexive project of the self', which is defined as 'the process whereby identity is constituted by the reflexive ordering of self-narratives' (Giddens, 1991, p. 244). In turn, the narrative of the self is defined as 'the story or stories by means of which self-identity is reflexively understood, both by the individual concerned and by others' (p. 243). Individuals understand themselves, construct their self-identity, by working and reworking their interpretation of their own biography in the form of a narrative or story. The result is 'a trajectory of the self', a path of development from the past to an anticipated future. The narratives that individuals construct are inherently fragile and have to be worked at continuously. 'A self-identity has to be created and more or less continually reordered against a backdrop of shifting experiences of day-to-day life and the fragmenting tendencies of modern institutions' (p. 186). Giddens makes clear that part of the construction of self-identity is a systematic ordering of the *body* – the control of shape, fitness, diet. The general point concerning reflexivity and our more specific rendering of the concept of narcissism are clearly very closely related. They both involve a reflection on the self in relation to others in imagination, whether that is by means of a narrative or a single image.

People are presenting themselves to others and, in doing so, are imagining how the others will see them. They are, in other words, performing for an imagined audience. Narcissism therefore provides the individual and motivational side of specatacle. In order to make the social world into spectacle, people have to be seen as the objects of spectacle. They have to be incited, motivated, to perform. Spectacle and narcissism are really two sides of the same coin. Both are effectively the consequences of the diffusion of performance out of its originally relatively confined settings. More of the events in everyday life are performances for which there is an audience. At the same time, more people see themselves as performers being watched by others; narcissism is the treatment of the self as spectacle.

POSTSCRIPT: AUDIENCES AND CONSUMERS

So, if the world has been turned into a series of spectacles involving performances, then it is also a world of *commodities*. In the way in which we intend to use the idea, commodification is a process with two principal aspects. First, it involves turning objects, events and services into *commodities*, that is, entities capable of bearing a financial value and of being traded in a market of some kind. Second, it involves the construction of individuals as *consumers*, that is, individuals for whom a central life-interest lies in the consumption of commodities. Clearly, these two aspects are intimately related; they are the supply and demand sides of commodification. The successful transformation of objects into commodities depends on there being willing consumers for those commodities. In turn, a career as a consumer can only be founded on a flow of suitable commodities.

The processes of commodification and of the creation of diffused audiences are connected because, at the same time as the world becomes a diffused audience, members of that audience also become consumers. Actually this last is a double process. On the one hand, all culture becomes a commodity, while, on the other, all commodities become aestheticized. We have already discussed both these processes. As for the first, the production and consumption of cultural objects and events are increasingly subject to the processes of commodification. As far as the latter is concerned, commodities are acquiring sign-value as well as exchange-value. Producers and consumers collude in aestheticizing commodities. Indeed, in an aestheticized world, commodities can only be sold if they self-consciously trade on their aesthetic value.

The effect of these processes is that audiences become markets and all markets are constructed as audiences. The twin processes of commodification and aestheticization are further deepening the diffusion of audiences. So, the diffused audience is becoming a market for cultural goods, while markets only work because consumers (and producers too) are increasingly treated as members of an audience. Indeed, in an aestheticized and commodified society, consuming is like being a member of a diffused audience because both involve *performance*.

This discussion of commodification prompts one further set of reflections which bring us back full circle to the issue of power and to the relationship between two of the paradigms described at the beginning of this book. One of the features of markets is that they are corrosive of the traditional bases of power and authority. Markets contribute to that fragmentation of power that we noted earlier in this chapter. It is not, therefore, that questions of power are altogether missing from SPP but only that they are assigned a lower priority than they receive in the IRP. That there are power relations in society is really, for the SPP, a subsidiary issue deriving from more important ones.

In this chapter we have argued that one way in which the diffused audience is constructed is via the relationship of Spectacle and Narcissism. To say that the world is conceived as a series of spectacles is to say that it is treated as something to be attended to. No longer can people, objects, or events be simply taken for granted; they are instead constituted as performances which command audiences. At the same time as the world is full of performing entities, the characteristic personality structure of contemporary societies is narcissistic. In the sense in which we use it, that means that individuals see themselves as performers in front of an imagined audience.

Spectacle and Narcissism are thus mutually reinforcing. Both demand and produce performances. Individuals are seen as performers and see themselves in the same light. Spectacle and Narcissism constitute a circuit.

4

Imagination and Resources

In the last chapter we argued that there is a circuit of spectacle and narcissism (the circuit of S–N–S), the nodes on this circuit being *performances* of one kind or another. If, increasingly, the world is conceived as spectacle, then so are the people within it. People see others as performers and come to see themselves as performers. Everyone acts as if they are performers for an audience yet they are also an audience for others. There is therefore a continuous flow of events, experience and perceptions round the spectacle/narcissism circuit. This flow requires a certain energy to drive it and the people involved have to have the resources necessary continually to renew the processes of spectacle and narcissism. In this chapter we discuss the mechanisms by which the S–N–S circuit is sustained. The most important of these mechanisms is imagination, which is required both to be a narcissist and to construct the world as spectacle. If imagination is the fuel of the circuit, so to speak, then it works only because it is *socialized*. That is, a critical component or object of imagination is the presence of *others* – an imagined community which acts as the audience in the mind for narcissism and spectacle. Lastly, imagination requires resources for it to operate successfully, and the most important resource is the media. As the media are omnipresent in modern society, so also is the S–N–S circuit peculiarly modern.

IMAGINATION

A world of spectacle, narcissism and performance requires the power of imagination. The diffused audience requires audience members to deploy considerable *imaginative resources*. Of course, simple and mass audiences ask people to use their imagination. Confronted with *Macbeth*, audiences have to imagine what it is like in a Scottish castle. When watching *Coronation Street*, audiences have to picture real buildings in Salford, rather than the artificial set that is in fact used. But in the case of diffused audiences the process goes much further. In order to appreciate the entire world as spectacle, in order to take in an aestheticized world in which symbols play an enhanced role, people must exercise their imagination more fully. Similarly, in order to be an accomplished narcissist, imagination is a required resource. People have to imagine what it would be like to perform in a certain way by the manner of their appearance or taste, for example, and what the responses of others would be to that performance.

Some light can be thrown on these processes of imagination by a consideration of Campbell's book *The Romantic Ethic and the Spirit of Modern Consumerism* (1987). Campbell's intention is to explain the *particular* character of contemporary consumer society – the spirit of modern consumerism. For him, there is something about the dynamic and insatiable quality of modern consumerism which sets it apart from the apparently similar consumerism of past societies. The challenge is to develop a theory that 'addresses the central question of how individuals manage to develop a regular and endless programme of wanting in relation to new goods and services' (p. 58).

Campbell's argument begins from a distinction between traditional and modern hedonism. Traditional hedonism is essentially based on appeals to the senses. At its most basic this involves pursuits such as eating, drinking or sex. The difficulty is that these senses do not permit of much variety and are easily sated. Sensations based on the non-appetitive senses of hearing and sight, on the other hand, can be discriminated more finely, as in the arts for example, but are, at the same time, less exciting.

Although traditional hedonists may employ a number of devices to enhance the experience of sensation, the pleasure that they derive will be limited. Modern hedonism, on the other hand, has an entirely different basis. It is founded in *emotion* rather than *sensation*.

> That emotions have the potential to serve as immensely powerful sources of pleasure follows directly from their being states of high arousal; intense joy or fear, for example, produces a range of physiological changes in human beings which for sheer stimulative power generally exceed anything generated by sensory experience alone. (p. 69)

What is distinctively modern about emotional arousal is that it is internal and controlled.

> The central point to be emphasized in this context is that only in modern times have emotions come to be located 'within' individuals as opposed to 'in' the world. Thus, whilst in the contemporary world it is taken for granted that emotions 'arise' within people and act as agencies propelling them into action, it is typically the case that in premodern cultures emotions are seen as inherent in aspects of reality, from whence they exert their influence over humans. (p. 72)

The internalization of emotion is, in turn, generated by various cultural changes. One is Weber's disenchantment. The modern world is no longer full of magical possibilities to which individuals respond. Instead the enchantment is turned inwards. Another is the growth in the West of notions of individualism and individuality. As we showed in Chapter 3 the self is now a viable object of contemplation, as are the self's emotions.

For Campbell, people in modern societies can successfully adjust the nature and intensity of emotional experience through the skilful use of the faculty of imagination. While it is possible to use this skill to summon up physical sensations, it is much more easy to imagine *emotional* states and to gain pleasure thereby. A major characteristic of modern experience, therefore, is the use by individuals 'of their imaginative and creative powers to construct mental images which they consume for the intrinsic pleasure they provide, a practice best described as day-dreaming or fantasizing'

(p. 77). Such day-dreaming is a speculation about what the future holds but it is a pleasurable speculation which is separable from fantasy because it contains elements that are possible and realistic. Modern individuals may therefore day-dream about a future event, perhaps a wedding, in which their new clothes are perfect, the sun is shining and the wedding march is played perfectly. These speculations are pleasurable in themselves, but there is also pleasure in the knowledge that their realization is perfectly possible. It is worth noting at this point, contra Campbell, that fantasies and day-dreams are not easily separable but rather lie at opposite ends of a spectrum of imaginings. The fantasy analogue of the wedding day-dream described above might therefore be a marriage with the Prince of Wales at Balmoral. However, most people's day-dreams probably consist of an amalgam of fantasy and reality. Indeed, without an element of the unlikely or impossible, day-dreams will not carry the required emotional punch. A further distinction to note is that between fantasy and day-dreaming, on the one hand, and the transformations of self that may result, on the other (Stacey, 1991, 1994). Clearly, transformations of self that proceed from fantasy will excite more comment from others – the real and imagined audience for the performance. Someone who dresses like Marilyn Monroe and walks and talks like her may well be called a fantasist. On the other hand, most people try to transform themselves from time to time in accord with their more moderate day-dreams and, in doing so, may invite little or no comment from their audience.

The importance of imagination and day-dreaming lies, for Campbell, in their relationship to longing, desire and, ultimately, consumption. Day-dreaming leads to longing which issues in an act of consumption. Unfortunately, this is necessarily an unstable conjunction, for, despite the possibility of realizing day-dreams, most of them cannot be realized precisely, leading to another round of day-dreaming and subsequent consumption. Intriguingly, the account of narcissism as unmet desire gives a similar dynamic. For us, however, the significance of Campbell's argument lies in its relationship to the idea of diffused audiences. As he himself says of day-dreaming:

This is the distinctively modern faculty, the ability to create an illusion which is known to be false but felt to be true. The individual is both actor and audience in his own drama, 'his own' in the sense that he constructed it, stars in it, and constitutes the sum total of the audience. All this drastically alters the nature of hedonism, for not only does modern man take pleasure in his day-dreams, but obtaining enjoyment from them radically changes his view of the place of pleasure in real life. (Campbell, 1987, p. 78)

If imagination is a skill general to human beings, then day-dreaming is a specifically modern form of it. We deployed an analogous argument about performance in earlier chapters. Performance might be a very general feature of social life, but modernity involves a particular, and intense, form of it. The modern faculty of day-dreaming means that people are able to imagine themselves performing in front of other people and also imagine the reactions that others will have.

The connexions between imagination, day-dreaming, spectacle, narcissism and performance are illustrated by an account given by Ewen (1988) of his students' attitudes towards style generated by asking them to write an essay on 'What style means to me'. Generally speaking, the students thought of style – in clothes, taste, opinions – as a form of expression of what they wanted to be and what they wanted others to think of them. The adoption of a style is a series of performances which makes a spectacle of each student who imagines him- or herself as looked at by an appropriate audience. These performances are anticipated in what we are calling day-dreams.

> For some, style was part of the way that they 'imagined' themselves, entered into fantasies about themselves. Victoria T— spoke of 'style' as listening to classical music while studying, revealing, in the process, the hunger *to be an image* that some people experience. 'It's hard for me to explain,' she related, 'but it makes me feel like . . . it's background music to a movie I'm part of. Since my dreams and desires are of being in a movie, I feel pleasure and ease with classical music.' (p. 6)

We take this discussion of imagination further in the later stages of this book. However, somewhat anticipating the consideration of fans and enthusiasts in Chapter 5, it is significant that one of the

most commercially successful discussions of contemporary audiences and fandom (Hornby, 1992) begins by examining processes
of fantasy and day-dreaming. The author slips in and out of
fantasy while lying in bed in the morning, rehearsing and reliving
important points in football matches involving Arsenal. Moreover,
this activity is contrasted with thought, as defined in a rationalist
manner: 'None of this is *thought*, in the proper sense of the word.
There is no analysis, or self-awareness, or mental rigour going on
at all' (p. 10).

THE MEDIA AND IMAGINATION

As we have already said, mass audiences and, to some extent,
simple audiences are organized around discrete media events. As
the audience experience becomes more diffused and no longer so
concentrated on discrete events, the media continue to be important and take on additional functions beyond the provision of
performances for simple and mass audiences. That is, they function as well to provide a flow of images and experience which is
used by individuals in their daily lives. The daily performances
which constitute a spectacular and narcissistic society are frequently organized around media images of style, personality,
clothing, music, and so on. The aestheticized society which we
described earlier is therefore partly a media-impregnated society.
The media, in all their forms, have worked their way into daily life
on an unprecedented scale. In Chapter 2 we described the way in
which various media forms are infused into everyday life. Besides
being regulative or constitutive of everyday life, the media also
provide images, models of performance, or frameworks of action
and thought which become routine resources of everyday life.
People, in other words, *use* what the media provide in daily life. A
similar point is made by Urry (1990) in relating tourism to day-
dreaming. For him, tourists go to the places they do because

> there is an anticipation, especially through daydreaming and fantasy,
> of intense pleasures, either on a different scale or involving different
> senses from those customarily encountered. Such anticipation is con-
> structed and sustained through a variety of non-tourist practices, such

as film, TV, literature, magazines, records and videos, which construct and reinforce that gaze. (p. 3)

Urry makes the further important point, which we take up later, that this media-assisted day-dreaming is not a purely individualized activity but is socially organized, not least because the provision of mass media is socialized.

This omnipresence of the media is summed up in Appadurai's (1993) use of the term 'mediascape'. The word is very well chosen because, like landscape, it carries with it not only the sense of omnipresence, but also the notion that people are *immersed* in the media which are largely *taken for granted*.

Appadurai's starting point is the role of the imagination:

The world we live in today is characterized by a new role for the imagination in social life. To grasp this new role, we need to bring together: the old idea of images, especially mechanically produced images (as in the Frankfurt School sense); the idea of the imagined community (in Anderson's sense); and the French idea of the imaginary (*imaginaire*), as a constructed landscape of collective representations, which is no more and no less real than the collective representations of Emile Durkheim, now mediated through the complex prism of modern media. (p. 273)

The imagination is a *social practice* and is:

No longer mere fantasy (opium for the masses whose real work is elsewhere), no longer simple escape (from a world defined principally by more concrete purposes and structures), no longer elite pastime (thus not relevant to the lives of ordinary people) and no longer mere contemplation (irrelevant for new forms of desire and subjectivity), the imagination has become an organized field of social practices, a form of work (both in the sense of labor and of culturally organized practice) and a form of negotiation between sites of agency ('individuals') and globally defined fields of possibility. (p. 274)

The constitution of the imagination as a social practice is a *global* phenomenon. Persons and social groups around the world live in imagined worlds which are very different from one another and which are frequently in conflict. These imagined worlds are constructed from five 'landscapes' – ethnoscapes, mediascapes, technoscapes, finanscapes and ideoscapes – whose relationship, in Appadurai's view, is becoming increasingly disjointed. From our perspective, it is not so much the relationships between the five scapes in determining global cultural flows that is important, but rather the nature and function of the mediascape itself.

> Mediascapes refer both to the distribution of the electronic capabilities to produce and disseminate information (newspapers, magazines, television stations and film production studios), which are now available to a growing number of private and public interests throughout the world, and to the images of the world created by these media. (p. 278)

Mediascapes provide large and complex repertoires of images and narratives, convoluted mixtures of the world of news and the world of commodities, to people throughout the world. Out of these elements the audiences construct scripts of imagined lives, their own as well as those of others in far-away places, 'fantasies which could become prolegomena to the desire for acquisition and movement' (pp. 278–9). Mediascapes blur the distinction between the real and the fictional, and the further away people are from metropolitan life the more fantastic are the imagined worlds that they produce. One should also note that, for various different reasons, modern mass media may be more effectve providers of raw material for the imagination than simple audience forms, the theatre for example. This is not only because of the intensity of media exposure but also because of the mode of involvement. Horton and Wohl (1956), for example, argue that there is an intensity of involvement in theatrical performance for the duration of the show, but the moment the actors take their bows, they cross 'back over the threshold into the matter-of-fact world'. Television, cinema and radio, on the other hand, produce a continuous interplay between the two worlds of mundane reality and performance; they are 'alternately public platforms and theatres'. The result is a new kind of relationship, which Horton and Wohl call 'para-social', in which a bond of intimacy is struck up between medium and performer, on the one hand, and audience members, on the other. As our earlier discussion bears witness, television's domesticity reinforces these bonds of intimacy.

In arguing that the media provide the resources for the diverse and complex imagined worlds within which people will live, it is perhaps important not to claim too much. Within the intense mediascape that modern societies provide, there is much that is unregarded or discarded by audiences; it is not that every magazine article, piece of music or television programme is instantly taken in as fuel for the imagination. Hermes (1995) makes much the same point in arguing that not all media products are *meaningful* to the audience. What audiences are doing, therefore, is drawing from the endless media stream that passes them by a set of diverse elements out of which they can construct imaginative worlds that suit them. We have very little empirical evidence about the constitution of these worlds. It must be a fair guess, however, that they are socially constructed. In other words, the use of particular media resources for the imagination is not a random process. People will build particular imagined worlds around their previous experience and existing lives in the worlds of work, family and household and general social relationships (see Bagnall, 1996).

Clearly, the media can fuel the imagination in different ways and at different levels. Magazines produce recipes which give rise to the imagined perfection of a dinner party; advertisements for holidays generate day-dreams of sun and sand; television soap opera exemplifies human relationships which can be an imaginative resource; and films will use stars who provide a means of identification and fantasy.

It has long been claimed that cinema offers a 'reservoir of common ready made day-dreams' (Maltby and Craven, 1995, p. 22). Sometimes the cinematic experience is described as *escape*. People will use the publicly available fantasies of the cinema to escape from their dreary everyday lives. Perhaps even the narrative resolutions of films enable audience members to resolve conflicts in their own lives. From our point of view, the use of the word 'escape' is misleading. It is not precisely that the media provide the resources of escape from the mundane world but rather that they provide some of the materials for living within it.

One way in which films provide imaginative resources is via *identification* with stars. Again one should note that this exercise of the imagination in constructing day-dreams is more complex than at first appears. Stacey (1991), for example, shows that there is a multiplicity of ways in which audience members identify with film stars. There is, to begin with, a distinction between 'processes of identification which involve fantasies about the relationship between the identity of the star and the identity of the spectator' but contained within the cinematic context, and those 'which involve practice as well as fantasy, in that spectators actually transform some aspect of their identity as a result of their relationship to their favourite star' (p. 149). The first of these is, in turn, divided into several modes. First, audiences can worship stars who are treated as beings existing on another plane. The spectator only exists as a worshipper and there is no notion of closing the gap between star and audience. Second, spectators want to become the star or to become like the star. There is therefore a gap between the two but the spectator wants to close it or transcend it. Third, the spectator finds pleasure in the feminine power of the star and her glamour, confidence and personality. Fourth, the spectator wishes to escape by becoming part of the star's world, by obliterating the difference between star and spectator.

Practices of identification which involve going beyond day-dreaming to alterations of behaviour can also take different forms. Spectators can pretend to be like the star, perhaps in concert with others, but all the time knowing that it is a game. Alternatively, spectators can claim to resemble the star in some particular or other. This does not involve pretending but simply selecting some point of resemblance. Or audience members can imitate and copy their preferred star, dressing, talking or walking like her. In sum, in all these cases, film stars provide material for day-dreams in different ways, extending from imaginings to transformations of the self.

Magazines function similarly as a resource for imagination. Craik (1994) describes the way in which women's magazines have provided a changing notion of what it is to be feminine.

Nineteenth-century emphases on women's nature and duties have been replaced in the first half of the twentieth century by notions of women as home-makers – mothers, nurturers, expert cooks and interior decorators – and additionally in the second half by ideas of women as self-confident professionals with independent lives of their own. In addition, throughout the twentieth century, magazines have treated women as consumers for a whole variety of products. All this is to provide an endless resource for imagining effective performance. As Craik says of women's magazines throughout the twentieth century, 'On the one hand, they offer advice, informantion and instruction specifically for women (practical techniques of being female), while on the other hand, they offer images of femininity, fashion, and beauty (techniques of desire and femininity)' (p. 50). In an important recent study of women's magazines, Hermes (1995) similarly draws attention to the importance of day-dreaming and fantasy. She argues that the magazines provide resources for the construction of fantasy 'investments'. In particular, 'women's magazines offer material that may help you imagine a sense of control over your life by feeling prepared for tragedy, or a more perfect vision of yourself by supposing that you would be able to answer any question regarding the difficult choices someone else might ask' (p. 144). Thus, clipping recipes from a magazine may be an aspect of the imaginative construction of the self as a better 'home-maker', even if the recipes are never actually used.

Simply because television takes up so much more time than all other leisure pursuits combined, it is bound to be an important resource for day-dreams. It may be rather less overwhelming than would be indicated by this omnipresence, however. Paradoxically, while cinema, advertising and magazines provide powerful *visual* images, which are more crucial in conveying meaning and in giving the audience pleasure, television is actually rather more dependent on *talk* for its effect. As a medium it really consists of visually illustrated talk. This, indeed, may be one reason why television is so much more a writer's, and less of a director's, medium than cinema. Television is intended to be received in a domestic context which is characterized by conversational interchanges and it mirrors and interacts with the conversational lives

of its audience. Television has a particularly direct way of address-
ing its audience as if a conversation was taking place between the
people appearing on the set and those watching it.

In addition, quite a few television genres are essentially organized around conversation, including talk shows, soap opera and
situation comedy. For others, news and documentary for instance,
talk appears to be the major ingredient. Still others, including
police shows, do give more prominence to visual images. However, there is also evidence that people frequently do not attend to
the visual images on television, whatever kind of programme is
on, but instead treat television as a talk medium. For example,
Hobson (1982) shows that watchers of *Crossroads* are only half
watching the programme as they are frequently engaged in
domestic work at the same time. They are, however, *listening*, and
may give their full attention to the set only when something
interesting comes up.

Television is not only *composed* of talk, it also *promotes* talk. It is
the way that audiences process programmes through talk about
them that gives the medium its function as a resource for imaginings. As Taylor and Mullan (1986) point out:

> Although 'television conversations' may often be about the comings
> and goings of fictional characters or 'personalities', they provide ways
> of talking about a great many features of the world: sex, sin, retribu-
> tion and death. Indeed . . . in some cases it seems that television drama
> has only properly occurred, been thoroughly realized, when the plots
> and the moral messages they contain have been discussed and inter-
> preted and re-dramatized in the company of friends or mere acquaint-
> ances. (pp. 205–6)

Of course, talk about television may be between all kinds of
different people and in all kinds of different settings. It also takes
different forms. Liebes and Katz (1993) make a useful distinction
between *referential* and *critical* forms of television talk. When
people talk about what they have seen on television, they frequently relate events or characters to their own lives. For example,
in discussions of soap opera, viewers will interpret the behaviour
of one of the characters by noting his or her similarities to
someone they know. The reverse may also happen, in that people
may interpret events in their own lives by reference to the way

that a television character behaves. Such uses of television talk may be termed referential – television refers to everyday life. Such referential talk can be contrasted with a critical mode in which the audience stands outside the television text. Critical talk will then be concerned with such features as how the programme is produced, whether the acting is any good, how the producers are managing cliff-hangers, whether the costumes are in period, or how the story-line is related to the need to gain good ratings. Several studies show that, when talking about television, audiences migrate backwards and forwards between referential and critical framings, as shown by the following example of television talk between young people from a study of audience reactions to *EastEnders* (Buckingham, 1987, p. 170):

> Calista: She's got to take the other people around her into considera-
> tion. I mean, it's her baby, it is her body, it is her life, but these other
> people, she's living with them, and they're the ones who've got to
> bear the brunt of whatever is happening. She's going to have this
> baby, and she's too young to have a baby, anyway.
> Donna: She's under age now, isn't she? She's still under parent
> guard.
> Sheila: I think it was wrong that she didn't tell her parents who the
> father is. Any parent is going to find out. Any parent is going to
> drag it out of them. I mean your parents know you better than
> anyone does. I think that the father should have the right to know. I
> mean it would bring out more in *EastEnders* wouldn't it?
> Calista: I suppose that they're saving it really, to use later on. And if
> their ratings go down, then they're going to use that to pick up their
> ratings.

It is chiefly in referential talk that audiences are in effect using television as an imaginative resource. Referential conversations between viewers of soap operas, for instance, represent a more or less seamless unity between references to experience and references to the characters in the soap; people bounce effortlessly backwards and forwards between their own world and the world of the soap opera. As Willis (1990) puts it:

> the young women who watch soaps are constantly judging them and
> reworking the material they provide, finding echoes in their own lives
> and spaces which allow them to ask what would happen 'if'. TV
> watching is, at least in part, about facilitating a dialectic between

representation and reality as a general contribution to symbolic work
and creativity. (p. 36)

If audiences use their experience to illuminate their television
watching and talk, they also do the reverse and use situations or
insights from television in their everyday lives. Adults may make
comparisons between a real-life event and one that has occurred
on television in order to manage their relationships. Children may
use television programmes to investigate and discuss the secrets
of the adult world (Buckingham, 1987). These occasions of the use
of television can also be playful. For example, Palmer (1986)
conducted a study of a group of children who used the series
Prisoner: Cell Block H as a basis for games in the playground. The
children would re-enact or invent episodes of the programme,
sometimes involving a teacher in the playing of the role of prison
officer. Fiske (1987) points out that *Prisoner: Cell Block H* provides
the children with a ready-made way of understanding and playing through their experience of school, for, in certain respects,
schools and prisons are similar in the importance of authority,
rules and rebellion.

Television references are also used more seriously in everyday
work lives. Pacanowsky and Anderson (1982), for example, show
how police officers routinely employ such references when carrying out their duties. This happens in three ways. First, nicknames
drawn from police shows on television are used to provide a
commentary on their individual characteristics. Usually these
were used ironically, a televison character's name being used to
suggest the opposite of the officer's real character. Second, by
using the language of television cops, particularly in the way that
criminals or members of the public are described, policemen
dramatized their work, drafting the excitement of television into
their everyday work life. Third, policemen contrasted their own
daily routine with the way that a cop's life is dramatized on
television. This is a way of showing what police work is really like
to each other and to the public at large; that is, it is uneventful, the
distinction between good and bad is not easily made, and real
police do not take unnecessary risks.

Through people's engagement with the media and their talk with others about the media, resources are provided which enable performance in everyday life and which drive the S–N–S circuit. The media provide a resource for seeing the world spectacularly; they create the world systematically as spectacle. Simultaneously, they provide some of the raw materials for narcissism. People replicate in their own lives the performance–audience relationships of the media. Something of this role of the media is indicated in the notion of media amplification – the way that the media are attracted to certain public events and by concentrating on them further enhance their significance. Here is an account of the conflicts in Brighton in the 1960s between the Mods and the Rockers:

> In 1964, John Albon, now Assistant Chief Constable of Devon and Cornwall, was an 18-year old in Brighton. 'My remembrance of it wasn't so much of violence as hordes of young people running around and looking for the excitement that others were committing. We were like a huge mobile audience though, in fact, we were the main act,' he said. (*Guardian*, 21 May 1994)

The media made the riots – if riots they were – into a spectacle. As a result, the participants came to see themselves not only as an audience, but also as performers, but performers scrutinizing their own performance. These performances require acts of imagination, attempts to conceive of an imagined audience beyond those immediately present. The spectacle–narcissism circuit, in other words, is a hall of mirrors which involves *reflexive* performance.

Other theorists press the point further in arguing that contemporary society is so media-saturated that it is literally impossible to see the external world except through the filter of the media. It is often said that some soap opera viewers cannot tell fact from fiction. Some viewers, for instance, apply for jobs at the corner shop or at the Rover's Return in *Coronation Street*. Again, there have been cases of actors who play unpopular characters on television being abused, or even attacked, in the street. Less extremely, perhaps, people frequently appear to talk as if the characters in favourite programmes are real, a characteristic that can attract the derision of those less involved in the programme concerned. This apparent merging of fiction and reality is not unrelated to the claim that television is a supremely postmodern form which appeals to a new, postmodern, audience, for whom television defines reality. Actually, the evidence of the way in which audiences frame television programmes indicates that people manage their commuting from the reality of television to the reality of everyday life very easily. If anything, as we have seen, audiences judge the televisual reality by the reality of everyday life. Television watching is not pure escapism either, a flight from a dreary unsatisfying reality to a fantasy world. This may be an element of the appeal, but it is outweighed by the pleasure of *relating* the events and characters on television to everyday life.

THE AUDIENCE AS COMMUNITY

One of the consequences of the role of the imagination in the construction of diffused audiences is an altered relationship of the members of the audience to each other as distinct from the relationship between the audience and the performance. Since the claim is that everybody is a member of an audience for each other's performances most of the time, the relationship between members of the audience is clearly going to be of more importance.

In day-dreaming, people will imagine the presence of others who constitute the audience for their daily performances. Needless to say, these others are not just *any* others. They are significant others who are of like mind and have similar tastes and attitudes. One way of conceptualizing the relationship between people who form part of this imagined presence is to describe it as a *community*. Our claim is, therefore, that the diffused audience is an imagined community. In this sense we propose to follow elements of the definition of community offered in the literature on the topic. For example, Cohen (1985) suggests that 'a reasonable interpretation of the word's use would seem to imply two related suggestions: that the members of a group of people (a) have something in common with each other, which (b) distinguishes them in a significant way from the members of other putative groups' (p. 12). Similarly, in a survey of the literature on community, Crow and Allan (1994) argue that 'Community ties may be structured around links between people with common residence, common interests, common attachments or some other shared experience generating a sense of belonging' (p. 1).

The phrase 'imagined community' was invented by Anderson (1991), who was interested in the formation and nature of the nation-state and the ways in which it can be said to be a community, albeit an imagined one. The idea of the nation is very powerful and can mobilize a population's energy, loyalty and trust in a way few other institutions can. The nation is also a community in that there is a strong sense of belonging to a common entity and having a shared sentiment, history and purpose. Thus, Anderson argues that the nation is a community because 'regardless of the actual inequality and exploitation that may prevail in each, the nation is always conceived as a deep, horizontal comradeship. Ultimately it is this fraternity that makes it possible, over the past two centuries, for so many people, not so much to kill, as willingly to die for such limited imaginings' (p. 7). However powerful the sense of community is in the nation, it is not founded in personal relationships as a local community might be. You do not have to know everyone in the nation and there does not even have to be the possibility of such knowledge. Each member of the nation-community simply has to be able to imagine every other member. Indeed, Anderson believes that almost every community 'larger than primordial villages of face-to-face contact' (p. 6) requires such acts of imagination.

People must have the means to construct the nation as an imagined community. We have argued that the media play a crucial role in the construction of the diffused audience, not least because of the way in which they fuel the imagination. Anderson adopts a similar argument for the construction of the nation as an imagined community. Newspapers, for example, have upon their pages a great variety of stories from many sources not obviously linked together in any way. 'The arbitrariness of their inclusion and juxtaposition . . . shows that the linkage between them is imagined' (p. 33). There are two sources of the imagined linkage.

One is the coincidence of occurrence at the same time. The other lies in the relationship between the newspaper and the market. The newspaper is a kind of obsolescent book, out of date almost as soon as read. Yet this obsolescence creates a mass ceremony of common identity paradoxically performed not only in private, but also in the heads of the readers:

> Yet each communicant is well aware that the ceremony he performs is being replicated simultaneously by thousands (or millions) of others of whose existence he is confident, yet of whose identity he has not the slightest notion. Furthermore, this ceremony is incessantly repeated at daily or half-daily intervals throughout the calendar. What more vivid figure for the secular, historically clocked, imagined community can be envisioned? At the same time, the newspaper reader, observing exact replicas of his own paper being consumed by his subway, barbershop, or residential neighbours, is continually reassured that the imagined world is visibly rooted in everyday life. (pp. 35–6)

One of the advantages of Anderson's formulation is that the idea of community is no longer spatially localized. The feelings, social behaviours and sense of identity that are typical of community in his model do not have to apply exclusively to a bounded geographical area. A similar notion is implicit in Cohen's (1985) idea that community should be seen as 'belonging'. He objects to the notion that community should be seen as a structural or natural category. Rather it is category of meaning or, in our terms, category of imagination: 'the distinctiveness of communities and, thus, the reality of their boundaries, similarly lies in the mind, in the meanings which people attach to them, not in their structural forms' (p. 98). The significance of communities, in other words, lies in the way in which people think about their relationships with other people that they deem to belong to the same community. Critical to this process of imagination is some notion of a boundary between one imagined community and another. 'Community' is essentially a relational concept; communities are defined in relation to one another as well as by the quality of the relationships internal to the community. Therefore, the feeling of belonging critical to the sense of community is constructed as much by *not* belonging to some imagined entity as it is by belonging to one.

By definition, the boundary marks the beginning and end of a community. But why is such marking necessary? The simple answer is that the boundary encapsulates the identity of the community and, like the identity of an individual, is called into being by the exigencies of social interaction. Boundaries are marked because communities interact in some way or other with entities from which they are, or wish to be, distinguished. (p. 12)

These boundaries may be physical or legal, but they are more likely to be *symbolic*, determined by the meanings given by people to the patterns of social interaction concerned.

Anderson and Cohen are, therefore, arguing that communities are imaginative constructs marked by boundaries that are largely symbolic; the sense of belonging engendered by the imagined community is also a construction of identity (a topic taken up in the next chapter). We have argued that diffused audiences are imagined communities in much the same sense and also have the essential connexion with the formation and sustenance of identity. Our argument, however, goes a little bit further. For Anderson and Cohen the imagined community has *some* spatial and temporal location. That is, members are spatially organized (the nation, the locality) and are imagined largely as co-existing. There are, of course, some exceptions to this rule. Ethnic communities often have no specific geographical locale and a sense of the past and of tradition is often an important part of the way that communities are imagined. The diffused audience, however, as an imagined community, is to a much greater extent, though not entirely, freed from the constraints of space and time; members of the diffused audience can be imagined from any time and, even more, from any spatial location.

The imagined community as a diffused audience is, of course, not a unitary phenomenon. Not all members of that community are alike, not all are equally relevant, and not all are equally important. Perhaps the best way of conceiving of the structure of the community is as a series of concentric rings around the individual extending in space and time. Some light can be thrown on this issue by considering the work of phenomenologists who have invested a great deal of effort in trying to describe the structure of the life-world. For example, Schütz (Abercrombie

1980; Wagner, 1970) argues that the centre of everybody's life-world is the individual, and that concentric zones of temporally and socially structured knowledge are grouped around that centre. Closest to the self is a zone of directly experienced reality, and persons who come within that zone share a community of space and time with the self. The zone of direct experience is vivid, with each person experienced as being unique. Outside this zone is the zone of contemporaries who share a temporal, but not necessarily a spatial, location, and who are not experienced immediately. Knowledge of contemporaries is always indirect and impersonal, although the degree of anonymity will vary from person to person. It may indeed be better to see these two zones as ranged along a continuum of vividness and anonymity. One way of relating the idea of imagined community as a set of zones to the process by which people use the media to make sense of the world is to conceive of Schütz's inner zone as a 'talk community', 'interpretative community' or 'improvisational community' (Machin and Carrithers, 1996). While for more remote zones the media are an *abstract* resource for imaginings, for the inner zone they are more direct in that media output, magazines and soap opera, for example, is talked about and processed together with people who are seen frequently and who are, in Schütz's word, 'consociates'.

POSTSCRIPT: MEDIA COMPETENCIES

The capacity to day-dream is a *skill* that human societies have developed. As we have argued at a number of points so far, it is a skill whose deployment is crucially furthered by the development of a number of forms of mass media. The modernity of these processes is related to the modernity of the media. The media therefore provide many of the resources that make exercises of the imagination possible and pleasurable. In day-dreaming about a forthcoming wedding, for example, the content of the day-dream will be informed by countless elements taken from media performances, whether they be from film, television, drama or music.

Modern societies take the media so much for granted that it is easy to forget that the appropriation of the media also does involve the learning of skills of various kinds. In many ways that is very like the hidden nature of all the skills of everyday life (see Giddens, 1990). As Thompson (1995) points out:

> The use of a technical medium generally presupposes a process of codification; that is, it involves the use of a set of rules and procedures for encoding and decoding information or symbolic content. Individuals who employ the medium must have a mastery, at least to some extent, of the relevant rules and procedures. To have a mastery of these rules and procedures is not necessarily to be able to formulate them in a clear and explicit fashion; rather it is to be able to use them in practice. . . . (p. 23)

For example, the implication of much film theory is that film is actually much more complex than it looks; we are fooled into thinking it easy because it is so very taken for granted. Take the simple question of the point-of-view shot. The shot will jump from one person's point of view to another quickly and easily and some shots come from no character's point of view at all. Yet we, as audience, make sense of all this perfectly easily. It requires a great deal of skill to make a film which is this complex and it requires a great deal of skill to make sense of it as an audience member. The same is true of television. Flitterman-Lewis (1992) points out the complexity of the television message in the case of soap opera:

> Within the space of any soap opera program hour (minus the fifteen minutes for commercials) we can find an incredible variety and complexity of both shot setups and narrative subsegments [. . . type of shot, camera angle, character movement, and camera movement . . .] . Our vision is thus dispersed, fragmentary, and amplified. (p. 228)

Such a form requires a variety of skills and competencies.

First, there have to be *technical* skills which embody an appreciation of how an effect is created. They include, as far as television is concerned, the qualities of the acting, of how feeling is conveyed, the production values, the script, the costumes, the camera work and the direction. To the extent that audiences reveal these skills in their conversation about any television programme, they are using a critical coding, in Liebes and Katz's terms. Second, there are *analytical* skills which have to do with the analysis of the television text from within. These include a knowledge of the genre and a capacity to reflect on the way in which any particular programme conforms to generic conventions, knowledge of the customs of particular series, and competence in the logic and coherence of character and plot. Audience talk using these skills will mostly be critical but might also use referential codings. Lastly, there are *interpretative* skills which involve an interpretation of television texts from without the text, by comparing them with something else, either other texts or with 'reality' or everyday life. Audience talk here is mostly referential.

Although we have exemplified these skills initially from television, it is possible to perform the same exercise on other media. So, for music there are technical skills clearly. There are analytical skills including both generic and specific. Lastly, there are interpretative skills in testing the authenticity of the music or the way in which it represents a way of life, as for rap, reggae, indie, folk, for example.

The deployment of skills of various kinds is therefore crucial to the way that audience members utilize the media to resource their imaginings. In the next chapter we look at the question of audience skills and competencies from a different point of view.

5

Fans and Enthusiasts

One of the central arguments in this book has been about the transformation in the nature of audiences. In this chapter we illustrate this argument further by treating fans and enthusiasts as a form of skilled audience. Through fan activity – which clearly involves the deployment of imagination fuelled by the media in an imagined community – people are helped to construct particular identities. We have two additional reasons for introducing the topic of fans and enthusiasts. First, it can be suggested that much of the literature on fans, at least in its early stages, was driven by concerns which arose from the Incorporation/Resistance paradigm. Thus, for example, the studies were concerned to examine the way in which sectors of the audience were *active* in response to dominant forms of mass media. Moreover, it was also suggested that such activity represented a form of resistance to the dominant messages contained in texts which on the face of it represented forms of dominant ideology. These ideological messages would be overcome and transformed into new meanings by fans (for example, Jenkins, 1992a). However, it can be argued that ultimately such studies are better understood within the SPP not the IRP as demonstrating the construction of alternative fans' communities based on the generation of particular forms of identification and identity. Second, our discussion of the SPP has tended to be undertaken at a rather general level so far. Hence, in this chapter we wish to offer some degree of classification of the nature of contemporary audiences, by drawing on some of the insights of the literature on fans and enthusiasts. We also want to chart some of the possible movements that exist between different audience types and positions. In this chapter we explore these areas in some detail, summarizing some of the key findings of the relevant literature and drawing out the implications for the SPP. Our argument will develop in the following way. We begin with a discussion of fans and follow this with a consideration of the enthusiast. We then compare these with a view to pulling out the similarities and differences between them. Our view is that 'ordinary' audience members are more like fans and enthusiasts than might initially be thought and that, given the increased contemporary salience of media fan-like and enthusiast-like qualities, sociation patterns are increasingly likely to resemble some of the relationships identified in the fan literature. In particular, expanding upon some of our earlier discussion in Chapter 4, it is important to identify the nature of the skill mobilized by fans and enthusiasts. We shall argue that these skills lead fans and enthusiasts to be productive in two general senses: materially of things and meanings; and of identities. These two senses are discussed in some detail in the later parts of the chapter.

FANS AND FAN PRACTICES

The *Shorter Oxford English Dictionary* defines fan as follows: 'orig. U.S. 1889 (In earlier use fann 1682) (abbrev. of fanatic). An enthusiast (a keen spectator of a sport, in early use esp. baseball.' We all probably have commonsensical images of the fan in our minds and they would perhaps be linked by the idea of some kind of excess of admiration of an activity or star. Moreover, there has been a clear tendency for journalistic writing on fans to suggest that there is something wrong with being a fan. Fans are seen as fanatics (from the origin of the term) and deranged (Jenson, 1992, p. 9). Jenson (1992) maintains that the literature on fans has produced two models of the 'pathological fan'. First, there is the *'obsessed loner'*, 'who under the influence of the media has entered into an intense fantasy relationship with a celebrity figure. These individuals achieve public notoriety by stalking or threatening or killing the celebrity' (p. 11). An example might be Mark Chapman, the 'fan' who killed John Lennon. Second, there is the *'frenzied or hysterical member of a crowd'* (p. 11), shouting at a rock star or misbehaving at a sports match.

Jenson argues that these models of fans relate to general characterizations of the nature of society, similar to the descriptions of mass society or mass culture. As Jenson puts it:

> The literature on fandom, celebrity and media influence tells us that: Fans suffer from psychological inadequacy, and are particularly vulnerable to media influence and crowd contagion. They seek contact with famous people in order to compensate for their own inadequate lives. Because modern life is alienated and atomized, fans develop loyalties to celebrities and sports teams to bask in reflected glory, and attend rock concerts to feel an illusory sense of community. (p. 18)

Jenson contests this idea that there is something wrong with the fan by contrasting the traits of the fan with those of the high culture or academic 'aficionado'. She argues that many academics form attachments to their favourite writers or theorists which are just as obsessive as those the fan may feel for the pop star. However, the division of the world between fans and non-fans allows those who define themselves as non-fans to suggest that others are abnormal and thus to constitute themselves as the normal or the safe. For Jenson:

> Defining fandom as a deviant activity allows (individually) a reassuring, self-aggrandizing stance to be adopted. It also supports the celebration of particular values – the rational over the emotional, the educated over the uneducated, the subdued over the passionate, the elite over the popular, the mainstream over the margin, the status quo over the alternative. (p. 24)

Jenson argues that characterizing fans as 'other' in this way blocks analysis and proper understanding of how people actually interact with the media in contemporary society. In particular, once mass society or mass culture theory and their variants have been rejected as ways of understanding the contemporary nature of media and society, the reconstruction of the category of the fan allows the thinking of new models of the audience. In an important sense, this means that Jenson is developing a critique of an argument within the Behavioural paradigm, in that she is criticizing the ideas of immediate and drugged response entailed by the mass culture view.

An important part of our argument is the rejection of the labelling of fans, cultists and enthusiasts as in some way deviant or deranged. Further, we want to concur with writers like Fiske (1992) who have suggested that fan activities are actually more like those of 'ordinary' audience members than might once have been thought. In order to go beyond these dictionary or commonsense ideas of fans, it is important to examine some of the recent literature. In the initial stages of our discussion, we propose to explore two main groups of studies to introduce and pull out some of the core issues involved: fans of *Star Trek* and related science fiction television programmes and of popular music.

There have been several important discussions of television science fiction fandom. The most important and comprehensive of these are *Enterprising Women* by Camille Bacon-Smith (1992) and *Textual Poachers* by Henry Jenkins (1992a, see also Jenkins, 1992b). In essence, these studies concern the appropriation and re-using of television texts like *Star Trek, Blake's 7* and *The Professionals* as the basis on which to develop new cultural forms. So the women in Bacon-Smith's study as well as those discussed by Jenkins do things with such texts. They go to conventions on them, they dress up as characters from the shows, they write and perform 'filksongs' about them, they paint pictures of the characters, they produce music videos about them, and so on.

Jenkins (1992a), like Jenson (1992), argues against the conventional dominant characterizations of fans as 'comic', 'psychotic' or 'eroticized' and values the activities of fans against such myths. Drawing upon the work of de Certeau (1984), Jenkins argues that fans are involved in poaching activities, in that they appropriate and transform the meaning of particular media texts. This can bring them into conflict with the producers of these texts, who, for example, may be developing the programmes that the fans admire in directions which they do not like. Moreover, fans are nomadic in that they move across and between texts and read intertextually. Jenkins is also critical of de Certeau in arguing that he suggests that such activities are not transitory, that fans are not socially isolated from each other, and that importantly in the case of fans there is no radical separation of readers and writers.

Jenkins (1992a) examines the fans' characteristic mode of reception of texts. He argues, contra critics such as Grossberg and Ellis, that the fans draw texts 'close to the realm of lived experience' (p. 53) and consequently they are not simply glanced at or regarded in an 'indifferent' manner. Moreover, developing this idea of the focus on the text, Jenkins suggests that fans reread the texts many times and that they insert 'program information' into 'ongoing social interactions' (p. 53). Meaning is produced through close attention to the nuances of the text and through social interaction in the everyday life of the fans (see also Chapter 4).

In Jenkins' argument, fans are not unthinkingly accepting of what is produced for them. They are actually discriminating in their approach, even towards the series of texts which are their favourites. Hence, the fans are active in their appropriation of texts and in their critical understanding of them. Fans are also productive in a material sense.

Bacon-Smith devotes much discussion to the types of written text that are produced utilizing the characters and situations from the different series, though again her main focus is on *Star Trek*. In these texts, characters and situations from the series are placed in new situations and different 'universes'. Furthermore, new characters are introduced or ones who had only relatively minor roles are developed at much greater length and depth.

Bacon-Smith identifies four main genres of *Star Trek* writing (see also Jenkins, 1992a, and Penley, 1992). The first of these is the 'Mary Sue', which entails the introduction of a young woman into the crew of the *Enterprise* who manages to save the ship and its crew from disaster, but who perishes due to her efforts. This is often the first sort of story written by the developing *Star Trek* fan, and has become a relatively disliked form. The term 'Mary Sue' is often used in a negative sense, the phrase 'it's a bit of a Mary Sue' indicating disapproval.

The second type of writing is the 'lay Spock' (or someone else from the crew). This involves producing a story which places Spock in a heterosexual relationship, for example with Nurse Chapel, who is thought to be attracted to him. The third type of writing is the 'K/S' or 'slash' (see also Penley, 1992) which places Kirk and Spock in a homosexual relationship. The final type is 'Hurt/Comfort', which again often places two of the central characters into a close relationship. One of the characters suffers pain through a terrible injury and the other character is involved in caring for and comforting the injured friend. This genre is explained by Bacon-Smith to be particularly controversial amongst fans due, for example, to the distressing effects that reading about the severe pain inflicted on a much-liked character can have.

Importantly, these texts are often produced in a collective manner. One individual may be primarily responsible for the initial development of an alternative *Star Trek* universe, but this is then opened up for expansion by others who can fill in gaps and open up new possibilities in the story. In an important sense, the authorship of these stories is shared. Their production goes against the stereotype of the lone author at work in creating for an industrialized book market.

The fans studied by Bacon-Smith and Jenkins also engage in a variety of other cultural activities derived from the show which is their favourite. Their creativity and activity is not just in the written format, but can involve video production, painting, and so on. Overall, Jenkins (1992a, p. 278) emphasizes that fans are active in five different senses. First, fans are active in their 'particular mode of reception', which Jenkins characterizes as 'emotional proximity and critical distance'. Second, they are active in that they use a 'particular set of critical and interpretive practices'. Thus, it is important to note that fans do not simply absorb that which is pumped at them, and fans are 'far from being uncritical or sycophantic about their show. Rather they establish an aesthetic history of "classics" and "worst ever" episodes which circulate through the fanzines. This aesthetic is articulated quite self-consciously in their discourse about "continuity" and "programme structure"' (Tulloch and Jenkins, 1995 p. 147). Third, 'fandom constitutes a base for consumer activism' in that fans organize to attempt to influence the direction taken by the producers of their favourite texts, or to attempt to get discontinued series returned to the television screen. Fourth, fans are active in their production of alternative texts, placing characters from established series into new situations and new universes. Finally, fans are active in that they create 'an alternative social community'. We can suggest then, on the basis of the studies discussed so far, that fans are: *skilled* or *competent* in different modes of production and consumption; *active* in their interaction with texts and in their production of new texts; and *communal* in that they construct different communities based on their links to the programmes they like. Similar processes are described in the literature on pop fans.

There are now a number of studies of pop music fandom including Aizlewood (1994), Ehrenreich et al. (1992), Garratt (1994), Roberts (1994), Smith (1995) and Wise (1990). Significantly, the earlier studies were written in the main by women, and took a kind of confessional stance, often based in feminist ideas of the attempt to dissolve divisions between the public and the private in accord with the idea that the personal is the political.

For instance, Sue Wise (1990) documents the personal nature of the relation to a star. Examining her feelings for Elvis Presley in the context of her own development as a feminist, she argues that Elvis has normally been written about, by men, as a kind of 'butch god', whose 'expression of rampant male sexuality' (p. 391) was central to his appeal. This reproduced boys' sexual fantasies concerning 'his supposed ability to "lay girls" with ease and without consequence' (p. 392), and led to the celebration of the early Elvis by male writers. 'Although he had a career of over twenty years, male writers dwell upon only the first couple of these, when they can identify with the super butch sexual hero that they themselves have promoted and lauded' (p. 392). By contrast, it is after this initial period that Wise's connexions with Elvis began.

Wise details how she collected pictures and cuttings about Elvis and how she created her own space within a crowded household through her immersion in Elvis. Elvis acted as a friend. Wise suggests that her feelings for him were not concerned with sex or romance but rather those of 'warmth and affection' (p. 395). Elvis was like a 'teddy bear'. One of the general implications of Wise's discussion is that people may have related to Elvis Presley in a variety of ways. She argues that adopting such a 'relativist' view would go some way to overturning the dominant male ways of examining the meaning and audience appropriation of Elvis Presley. It is possible to recognize the complexity of these different appropriations and meanings through even a quick inspection of a book like *Dead Elvis* by Greil Marcus (1992), which identifies the ways in which numerous different images of Elvis Presley continue to circulate in a variety of media and is itself a document of Marcus's own fan feelings for Elvis, which come through in the discussions of Elvis in his earlier work (1991). More recently men have also begun to write about fan feelings, in part prompted by the commercial success of fan books like Nick Hornby's *Fever Pitch* (1992).

These accounts have a number of common features. First, and perhaps somewhat obviously, they are almost invariably written by white men, in and around their thirties.[1] A central theme in the accounts is the attempt to deal with masculinity, especially in what journalistically are often called 'post-feminist' times. They may be said to exhibit a form of postmodern masculinity.[2] This relates to the second feature to be emphasized, the self-reflexive nature of the accounts. The examination of self is central, but it is perhaps an examination of self which can only go so far, in that it tends to be retrospective – examining the self at an earlier stage of life (especially the teens and early twenties) which has presumably been left behind, though the traces remain in the construction of a particular personality and 'sensibility' (Grossberg, 1992a, 1992b). Third, and again following logically, the accounts tend to be autobiographical. They follow through, to different lengths, a period in the hero's life, where the obsession was at its greatest, and which can now be commented on with some degree of ironic detachment. There is a clear sense in which these accounts are narrating and reconstructing a sense of identity, where the *writing* of the self is of critical importance.

A critical problem in the development of this sense of self, construction of identity and narration of a life is that of attachment. This is pursued in a variety of different directions. The family is problematic. Thus, for example, Hornby (1992) locates the beginnings of his attachment to football in general, and

Arsenal in particular, to the time of his parents' divorce, when a social setting was needed for the weekend trips with his father – Highbury provided the place where some contact between father and son could occur, without any real need for interaction. Likewise, and movingly, O'Connor (1994) locates his attachment to the Boomtown Rats in the 'difficulties' of his family life, which are explicitly introduced in the first two pages of his account. Attachment remains problematic in later life, where it is more likely to be the difficulties of attachment to women, who are very different creatures from men, which are central. Again, the texts in question narrate some of these problems and issues.[3]

While attachments to family and to women are a key problem of these texts, the temporary resolution is found in the attachment to a group or singer. In an often ironic way this enables the male author of the fan account to perform exercises in discrimination, where the 'hip' (see further Thornton, 1995) is set out, but in such a way as to comment on the impossibility of remaining hip, or having been in the 'know' at the right time. Again, Hornby (1994) catches the theme most characteristically when he opens a fan account of his attachment to Rod Stewart with: 'You want the classic early seventies albums, I got 'em. The entire Al Green back catalogue, *Let's Get It On, There's No Place Like America Today, Grievous Angel, After the Goldrush, Blood on the Tracks.* . . . Unimpeachable classics, every one.' He continues almost immediately with, 'Sadly, however, I am that commonplace phenomenon, Reinvented Man. Most of the Al Green back catalogue I bought in the early Eighties, the Gram Parsons at university in the late seventies, the Curtis Mayfield from a car boot sale a few years ago, and so on' (p. 23).

What is particularly important about both of these two broad types of fan study at the moment is, first, that these activities are organized around stars or media images and representations. Even if fans get into other activity (such as video making), this still revolves around stars or images; likewise pop fan activities tend to be particularly structured by one star or group.[4] Hence, all the contributors to the above volumes write about a single artist rather than a type of music. While this obviously occurs, there would still seem to be very specific attachments within even generic fandom. Our first point about fandom then is that it tends to be media-focused and -organized.

Second, it is likely that fans are relatively heavy users, especially in relation to their own favourite show or artist. There is relatively little evidence to support such a hypothesis, though by implication it would seem logical that the kinds of fan knowledge that are examined and displayed in the above texts could only be gained through extensive immersion in the works which are the object of worship of the fan.[5]

Third, fans engage in a variety of communal activities. Thus, as we have already seen, the *Star Trek* fans attend conventions based around their favourite shows and are in touch with many other fans, often through the circulation of different forms of fan text. Likewise an important dimension of female fandom of pop stars is the way in which it allows the coming together of different individuals around one particular focus of attention (Garratt, 1984, 1994). Further, this kind of bonding is often seen as oppositional, not only to the producers of the programmes adored by fans, because the producers may be doing things with the show which run counter to fan desires, but also to the established social relationships with which the fans themselves exist. *Star Trek* fans may have to establish what Bacon-Smith calls 'female terrorist space' against those men who run the established and long-running science fiction conventions. Likewise, female pop fans may be attempting, like Wise, to find some space for themselves in the context of a crowded household.

Some of these dimensions of fan activity, that is, their textual productivity and reinvention of the media message in alliance with the use of media to create their own spaces, have tended to draw those working at the forefront of the IRP to their activities. However, as we have suggested and will go on to argue further below, whilst these dimensions are important, they can only be properly understood through their relocation in different sets of concepts. In this case there will be consideration of identity, as has been foregrounded in the account of the male fan writers above. However, before we can begin fully to substantiate these ideas, it is important to introduce and consider the other literature which has influenced our thinking in this respect: that on enthusiasms.

ENTHUSIASTS AND ENTHUSIASMS

As we have already seen, the dictionary definition of the fan links this with being enthusiastic. Before we can comment on the precise nature of this linkage, however, it is important to consider some of the recent writing on enthusiasms. As with the literature on fans, this is small but growing. One of the most important things to indicate about this area is its scale and extent, which has often been relatively neglected by social scientists. As Stebbins (1992) explains, this is also a serious activity, a notion which he builds into his definition of 'serious leisure' as 'the systematic pursuit of an amateur, hobbyist, or volunteer activity that is sufficiently substantial and interesting for the participant to find a career there in the acquisition and expression of its specialist skills and knowledge' (p. 3). One of the first books to report on that scale and nature of these groups in Britain was Hoggett and Bishop's (1986) *Organizing Around Enthusiasms*, which includes an important definitional discussion.

Hoggett and Bishop (1986) use the label 'communal leisure' to describe groups which 'are mutual-aid organizations whose ostensible purpose is a leisure or recreation activity. They are collectivities which are self-organized, productive and which, by and large, consume their own products' (p. 40). It is important to consider the different dimensions of this definition in slightly more detail.

First, Hoggett and Bishop direct us to the point that enthusiasms are collective; more importantly, they suggest that they are organized and that with some variation they tend to be self-organized. There is then a significant degree of mutual aid in this process. This leads to an emphasis by Hoggett and Bishop on the fact that enthusiasms involve reciprocity and forms of exchange. They examine a number of different dimensions of production and consumption in this context. Thus, the enthusiasts are involved in production of various types, from that of particular things like plants in a gardening club, to plays in amateur dramatics, to the performance in a match by a football club. These products are consumed in the main by the members of the club, or similar enthusiasts who may belong to other clubs, or by the family and friends of the enthusiasts. Hence, goods are not produced for a market, or wider consumption, but for immediate use. Importantly, further, Hoggett and Bishop suggest that these activities are very important in the construction of the identities of the enthusiasts and the enthusiasm itself. The important components of these communal leisure groups are then 'collectivity, self-organization, production for self-consumption, mutual aid' (p. 42).

There are clear parallels between this definition of enthusiasm and that of the fan. Thus, both groups can be seen to be collective and to be productive in a context where consumption tales place by those who are also fans and enthusiasts. However, three important differences can be identified, which are further discussed below. First, enthusiasts' activities are not based around media images and stars in the way that fans' activities are. Second, the enthusiasts can be hypothesized to be relatively light media users, particularly perhaps of the broadcast media, though they may be heavy users of specialist publications which are directed towards the enthusiasm itself. Third, the enthusiasm would appear to be rather more organized than the fan activity. It is important to explore this issue of organization in rather more detail. An important source on this topic is the work of Moorhouse (1991).

In the context of a book-length study of the American hot-rod enthusiasm, Moorhouse develops a general model of the organization of an enthusiasm. He suggests that an enthusiasm will consist of a number of layers around a core. The core is made up of two main groups: professionals and amateurs (see also Stebbins, 1992). The professionals, those who make a living from the enthusiasm, are also referred to as the 'hot rod economy' (p. 22). This includes 'paid practitioners of the core activities, but also the "experts" of the enthusiasm of all kinds – administrators, officials, promoters, suppliers, dealers, writers' (p. 22). An important subgroup within this economy is the 'hot rod apparatus', who are the 'intellectuals' of the economy, owning or controlling the means of communication about the enthusiasm.

Amateur enthusiasts are also members of the core in Moorhouse's model. They are greatly involved with the enthusiasm and may in some respects operate as the kind of conscience of the professionals, perhaps being in conflict with some of the more commercial activities of the professionals in the enthusiasm's economy (see also Stebbins, 1992). Around the core of the enthusiasm is the 'interested public'. This consists of a 'heterogeneous group consisting of dabblers in the focal concerns, mere consumers of symbols, novices and new entrants, state bodies concerned with control, big businessmen seeking opportunities, the mass media looking for stories and so on' (p. 22). Outside this ring or layer there is the general public.

Specifically, Moorhouse suggests it is important to realize that the participants in the enthusiasm are actors in a process of change and that individuals can move from one sector to another over time. We shall have more to say on this later in the chapter. Diagrammatically we can represent Moorhouse's model as shown in Figure 5.1.

Moorhouse constructs his structural or topographical model of an enthusiasm in the context of a critique of theories of subculture.

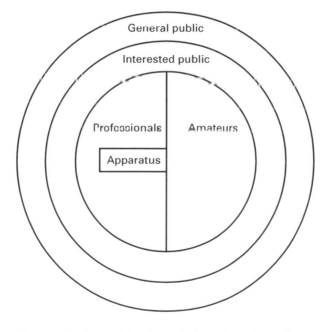

FIGURE 5.1   *Representation of Moorhouse's (1991) model of the American hot-rod enthusiasm*

However, it does share certain similarities with it, especially in the separation of three layers based on commitment to the enthusiasm. Many representations of subcultures are similar in that they are based on the separation of the true and committed subcultural adherents from those who are simply weekenders (Clarke, 1990; Thornton, 1995). Furthermore, it may be that it is difficult to capture the complexity of an enthusiasm and the way in which individuals move through it by this kind of model on its own. To develop this point we need to consider some discussions of subculture in rather more detail.

SUBCULTURE

There is now an extensive literature on this topic (for summaries see Baldwin et al., 1998, and Brake, 1985), much of which arose from consideration of 'deviant' subcultures and the spectacular youth subcultures studied from Birmingham in the 1970s. These literatures have been subjected to an important critique by Fine and Kleinman in a discussion which will be incorporated into the argument being developed here.

Fine and Kleinman (1979) argue that the concept of subculture needs to be rethought within a symbolic interactionist framework. Their approach is critical of the sort of work associated with the Birmingham Centre which placed emphasis on the structural aspects of society in the determination of subcultures. Further, they argue that the concept of subculture had previously been used in a confused and unclear fashion. They identify four conceptual problems with this literature: first, concerning the relationship between subculture and subsociety; second, with respect to the empirical referent of the subculture; third, in the characterization of the subculture as a homogeneous and static system; and, finally, in the value orientation adopted in subcultural research.

With respect to the first point, they argue that because of the way in which they have been structurally defined 'as aggregate of persons', subcultures have often been treated as a subdivision of society, or as what they call a subsociety. However, in contemporary societies, which allow movement between different groups and which have a number of different belief systems, it is difficult to see subsociety and subculture as the same thing. As Fine and Kleinman explain:

> Thus, all members of the age category 13–21 might, according to a 'structural' conceptualization, be considered part of the youth sub-culture. However, it is clear that many of the persons within that age cohort do not share common cultural values and behaviors. (p. 3)

On this basis, Fine and Kleinman argue that it is important to distinguish between subsocieties and subcultures.[6]

Concerning the second issue, they argue that the concept of subculture is often used without a referent – 'a clearly defined population which shares cultural knowledge' (p. 4). Thus, as they explain:

> Although researchers identify the subculture to which the group 'belongs' (such as the delinquent subculture), they have no way of knowing the extent to which the cultures of the gangs overlap, the extent to which the particular gang examined is representative of all gangs in the population segment, and the degree of interrelatedness among the cultures of the gangs under study. (p. 4)

The third point is more familiar in that Fine and Kleinman argue that the study of subcultures tends to treat them as if they were both homogeneous – more or less as if all members of the group were the same and all shared exactly the same beliefs and practices – and unchanging. In fact what should be kept in view is the fluidity of subcultures. Finally, they argue that through the selectivity of the way in which the subculture is discussed, the representation of it often becomes little more than a caricature. There is a tendency to focus on the central themes of the sub-culture, as in the work of Miller (1958) on deviant subcultures, at the expense of the complex interplay of different cultural aspects which may co-exist.

Fine and Kleinman argue that there is a better way to under-stand subcultures, proposing that 'the conceptualization of the subculture construct within an interactionist framework will pro-vide a more adequate account of subcultural variation, cultural change, and the diffusion of cultural elements' (p. 8). Therefore, they maintain that their approach overcomes the problems of earlier approaches. They argue that subculture should be used to refer to an interacting group. On first sight this would seem to produce rather small subcultures. However, Fine and Kleinman argue that subcultures exist beyond immediate groups because of the way in which cultural patterns are diffused in contemporary societies. The network which results from the diffusion of cultural elements is then the referent which they argued did not exist in most earlier writing. Subcultures start from group cultures:

> Cultural forms are created through the individual or collective manipulation of symbols. From its point of creation, the cultural form is communicated to others, and diffused outward from the individual's own interaction partners. The transmission of culture is therefore a product of interaction. The diffusion may remain quite limited unless the information reaches wider audiences via the mass media. (p. 9)

Fine and Kleinman identify four mechanisms by which communication can occur: first, individuals may be members of a number of different groups; second, there may be other interconnexions which do not involve group membership as such but which are based on 'weak ties', casual conversations with acquaintances and so on; third, some individuals or groups perform what Fine and Kleinman refer to as structural roles, in linking groups that may not otherwise be in contact and providing cultural information (drug dealers, for example); and, fourth, there may be media diffusion, as when certain films or television programmes influence cultures in the wider sense. This type of conceptualization of subculture can be seen as a specific instance of the characterization of the imagined community, as understood through the framework of Schütz, which was developed in the previous chapter.

Fine and Kleinman also emphasize the need for analysis to concern itself with what they call the 'affective' dimension of subcultures (p. 12). People need to be seen as involved in choices about culture and the extent of the identification with the culture needs to be considered and researched. An example of this approach can be found in Fine's (1983) book on fantasy gaming, which provides extensive detail on the social characteristics of gamers, in producing an account of a subsociety. Furthermore, Fine considers and emphasizes both fantasy and forms of identification in the production of the collective fantasy of the game. The concern with the social construction of a shared fantasy is of particular significance to the general argument concerning imagination that we have been making during the course of this book.

At least three general aspects of Fine and Kleinman's approach are important for our present purposes: first, the emphasis on concrete interacting networks; second, the emphasis on process and social change; and, third, the voluntarism which accords people choices in pleasures. These points have been developed in a rather different way by Thornton (1995) in her consideration of 'club cultures' from within a 'Bourdieu paradigm' (see further Longhurst and Savage, 1996) which emphasizes the role of distinctions in contemporary youth cultures. Moreover, Thornton (1995, p. 8) emphasizes the empirical approach of her work as distinct from the theoretical driven 'readings' of the Birmingham approach. In addition to this emphasis on empirical research and examination of distinction, Thornton's attention to the role of media in the generation and reconstitution of club culture is important. She examines the clubbers' own use of the critique of the media in the construction of their own senses of self and authenticity, but suggests that this neglects the very concrete use of different media, and that, like the academic writers on subculture from Birmingham, it relies on a problematic notion of the media and the mainstream. It is the centrality of the media in the construction of contemporary taste cultures which is important to emphasize in accord with the themes we have been developing in this book.

On the basis of these points, and the discussion hitherto, we want to suggest a set of terminological distinctions which involve the redefinition of some of the terms used in the studies discussed in this chapter so far. This terminological redefinition will enable further consideration of the areas of process and change, both on the individual and collective dimensions.

FANS, CULTISTS AND ENTHUSIASTS

Our suggestion is that the literature discussed so far can be read so as to introduce three categories ranged along a continuum: fan, cultist (or subcultist) and enthusiast, who are members of fandoms, cults (or subcultures) and enthusiasms respectively. These are different in some respects from the ways in which these categories are used in the approaches so far considered. Hence, in this section we shall spell out our understanding of them. In different ways all these individuals and groups are involved in production and consumption along different dimensions and we shall explore the similarities along these lines below. However, they do differ significantly along the dimensions of object of focus, extent and nature of media use and degree and nature of organization. The differences are summarized in Figure 5.2.

With the rider that we are in the initial stages of constructing a continuum here, which will be further developed below, the figure suggests the following. Fans are those people who become particularly attached to certain programmes or stars within the context of relatively heavy mass media use. They are individuals who are not yet in contact with other people who share their attachments, or may only be in contact with them through the mechanism of mass-produced fannish literature (teenage magazines, for example), or through day-to-day contact with peers. For example, many young children are fans. They tend to be relatively heavy TV viewers and form clear attachments which are constructed and reconstructed through day-to-day contact at school.

Cultists (or subcultists) are closer to what much of the recent literature has called a fan. There are very explicit attachments to

	Fan	Cult	Enthusiast
Object	Star/programme	Specialized star/programme	Activity
Media	Heavy	Heavy but specialized	Specialized
Organization	None	Loose	Tight

FIGURE 5.2   *Fans, cults and enthusiasts*

stars or to particular programmes and types of programme. In moving on from fans the cultist focuses his/her media use. They may still be relatively heavy users but this use revolves around certain defined and refined tastes. The media use has become more specialized, but tends to be based on programmes which, and stars who, are in mass circulation. The specialization also occurs through the increased consumption (and generation) of literature which is specific to the cult. Thus, as the studies discussed above show, increased immersion in fannish (in our terms cultist) literature occurs as the cultist becomes more involved. Given the constraints of time, we would expect this to cut down on the consumption of other material. Cultists are more organized than fans. They meet each other and circulate specialized materials that constitute the nodes of a *network*. In our terms, then, cultists are linked through network relations which may take a number of forms, but which are essentially characterized by informality. Such informality may often exist in spaces which oppose the dominant forms of organization of an activity. These more dominant forms often take the form of enthusiasms.

Enthusiasms are, in our terms, as we have already suggested, based predominantly around activities rather than media or stars. Media use is then likely to be specialized in that it may be based around a specialist literature, produced by enthusiasts for enthusiasts, even though the producing company may be part of a conglomerate. Furthermore, given the amount of time devoted to the enthusiasm by its participants, there is likely to be little time left over to sleep let alone read/view other mass-circulated texts. Finally, enthusiasms are relatively organized, in the ways suggested by Moorhouse, for example. In many respects the activities of those previously considered to be fans of *Star Trek* are actually closer to being enthusiasts.

Enthusiasms are sometimes contested by fans and cultists in particular. Thus, the women fans (or cultists) discussed by Bacon-Smith and Jenkins struggle against the male dominance of the SF enthusiasm and the fantasy role gamers discussed by Fine (1983) are criticized by the more established war gamers of an older generation. The organization of enthusiasms is a prime site for struggle and change.

AT THE ENDS OF THE CONTINUUM

Our argument, then, is that the categories of fan, cultist and enthusiast can be distinguished from other categories of person which exist at opposite ends of the continuum established so far: the consumer and the petty producer. In terms of the criteria which we have used in the elucidation of this continuum until now, consumers have a *relatively* generalized and unfocused pattern of media use. Of course they may have tastes, but these are relatively unsystematized. The extent of their media use may vary; it may be heavy, but it may not. In the sense that they are consumers, rather than fans of any one text, they are unorganized with respect to media use, and their organization as media users will not differ significantly from other aspects of social organization. However, it is important to stress our earlier contention that media are becoming more important in social organization for everybody.

At the other end of the continuum are the petty producers, who in a seeming paradox tend to turn the continuum into a circle as they become more like consumers. Petty producers are those who have perhaps developed from being enthusiasts to become a professional in Moorhouse's terms. Thus, the car enthusiast who begins to be concerned with the production of specialized parts may be on the route of moving from being an enthusiast to becoming a full-time producer where the previous enthusiasm becomes a full-time occupation. Pop music is especially interesting in this respect, and we shall examine it through the work of Shank (1994) in Chapter 6. This will lead to the use of even more specialized literature which may become ever more technical, involving the knowledge of British standards, patent law or copyright law, for instance. Finally, relationships tend to become organized through the market, and are therefore outside the control of the group of enthusiasts. As the enthusiast moves out of an enthusiasm towards being a petty producer or forms a production company, he/she is returned more to general capitalist social relations; as producers, they are as much at the mercy of structural forces as the consumers at the other end of the continuum.

```
Consumer—Fan–Cultist–Enthusiast—Petty Producer
```

FIGURE 5.3 *The audience continuum*

An important part of our argument is that we have identified a synchronic and diachronic continuum in the audience, which is represented in Figure 5.3. Lest we be misunderstood, it is important to stress that we are not making judgements about the relative worth of these different positions along the continuum. In our view there is not necessarily more worth in being an enthusiast than a consumer.

Our approach here chimes with some other recent accounts. Thus, in their consideration of science fiction fans, Tulloch and Jenkins (1995) make a distinction between fans and followers, in the following terms:

> This book will, therefore, adopt a distinction between fans, active participants within fandom as a social, cultural and interpretive institution, and followers, audience members who regularly watch and enjoy media science fiction programmes but who claim no larger social identity on the basis of this consumption. Fans and followers are conceived as two specific segments of the larger science fiction audience, though the boundary between the two groups remains fluid and somewhat arbitrary. (p. 23)

Perhaps to emphasize the fluidity and differential extent of consumption, Tulloch and Jenkins also talk of those 'secondary followers' like 'young mothers' in the audience remembering 'their pleasures and fears in *Doctor Who* from childhood, and, in the present, keeping regularly, but probably distractedly abreast with the series while cooking tea for their children' (p. 113). Our suggestion is that consumers are increasingly *follower*-like in their tastes, as society becomes more media-saturated.

While we have suggested in our discussion so far that we have been identifying a continuum, it can also be suggested that this continuum may represent a possible career path under certain conditions. This is an area importantly investigated by Stebbins

(1992), who traces a potential progression from amateur to professional, through five stages: 'beginning, development, establishment, maintenance, and decline' (p. 70). The beginning is fairly straightforward in that it characterizes the start of the progression. Development is the stage of more systematic engagement with 'serious leisure'. Stebbins identifies five 'patterns of development': sporadic, gradual, steady, broken-steady and delayed-steady. Different patterns of development tend to occur in different activities. Thus Stebbins found, for example, that stand-up comedy most commonly fell into the steady pattern. As might be expected, there are a number of 'contingencies' built into the development of the career, to do with geographical location, for instance. Moving beyond the 'learner' stage leads to 'establishment'. Reactions to parents can have a significant role at this point in determining between the subsequent development of an amateur or professional career path, as can the decision to go commercial (see, classically, Becker, 1963, and further Longhurst, 1995). The fourth stage is maintenance, where the 'amateur-professional career is in full bloom' (Stebbins, 1992, p. 88). This is the time of greatest career rewards, but it is followed by career decline in the final stage.

THE DIFFERENTIAL DISTRIBUTION OF SKILLS

In Chapter 4 we distinguished three types of skill or competence: technical, analytical and interpretative. Technical skills embody an appreciation of how the textual effect is created. For television, these include evaluation of acting, conveyance of feeling, production values, script, camera work. These apply to other media as well; hence, for popular music, they include performance, conveyance of feeling, production values, writing/construction of the piece, production work, and so on. Analytical skills have to do with the analysis of the text from within the parameters of the text itself. These include: generic (soap opera, reggae), corpus-specific (knowledge of *Coronation Street*, the Bob Marley corpus), personification/characterization (Is someone acting in character? Are rounded characters created? Does the music create coherent images?), plot/narrative (Does it work? Is it coherent?). Interpretative skills are to do with the interpretation of texts from without the text, by comparing them with something else. These include: inter-text comparisons (is *Coronation Street* better than *EastEnders*? How does k.d. lang play off Patsy Cline? . . .) and comparisons with reality or everyday life (How real is *Coronation Street*? Does Ice Cube articulate the community feelings of Compton?). As the examples show, we apply these skills to different media. How do these categories of skill map on to the continuum developed above?

A summary of the distinctions here is contained in Figure 5.4. It is worth pointing out, before we say any more about these distinctions, that in general levels of skill increase over time after the introduction of a particular media form. With regard to technical skill, our view is that the consumer will have very specific technical skills. He or she will be able to assess some aspects of technique, but will have relatively little background knowledge about the reasons for such judgements. For example, much daytime soap opera in Britain is routinely criticized for bad acting or poor sets, without appreciation of the relatively low production values which generate such drama. These judgements are clearly made, and can be argued to be 'accurate' in that the sets in *Neighbours* may look unreal, for example, but they are decontextualized and relatively unsubstantiated – they are assumed. It is the filling in of contextual knowledge which develops such technical skills. Thus, the fan, through his or her reading and discussion with others, fills in the context which enables him or her to come to fuller and more reasoned technical judgements. Fans of a particular band may know that a poor performance was due to the star having an illness, for example. This is the sort of knowledge that is increasingly available in mass circulation press and magazines. The cultist has even more of such knowledge, which is filled in through the narrow-cast media which circulate within the cult itself. Thus, royal watchers (Rowbottom, 1994) will explain the appearance of members of the royal family through very specific and precise information (or their interpretation of such information) which would not be mobilized by the general public. Furthermore, the cultist makes the transition into using such

Skill	Consumer	Fan	Cultist	Enthusiast	Petty producer
Technical	Very specific	More context, especially of stars	More context, move into the use of such skills	Increased use of such skills, in production for enthusiasm	Use of skill in production for market
Analytical	Very generalized	Within genres or comparisons	Immersion in genre and intrageneric comparisons	Immersion leads to increased productivity	Comparisons to locate market niches
Interpretative	Referential mode, taste in consumer purchase	Generic and used in fan legitimation	Use in authenticity arguments	Immersion leads to less outward direction	Comparison for profit

FIGURE 5.4   *The skills continuum*

technical skills in the production of texts of his/her own. The cult video maker will have a developing knowledge of video techniques, for example. This use of technical skills is further developed by enthusiasts, who are moving from the reading or viewing of other people's texts to the production of their own within an enthusiasm, for example the photography or gardening enthusiast. It is the use of skills that becomes paramount. This is then further developed when the enthusiast becomes a petty producer. In particular, specific technical skills (how to make a video, for example) need to be allied to skills which are more general: how do you market a video or distribute a record? The petty producer uses technical skills, but because of the market context needs to learn skills beyond those found in an enthusiasm.

In general, then, it is possible to see an increase in technical skills across the continuum. It is important to emphasize, however, that such skills are becoming increasingly prevalent amongst consumers. Take video production, for example, where, though they may be less skilled than fans, cultists or enthusiasts, consumers possess skills in this realm that would have been unthinkable ten years ago, primarily due to the technological innovation in camcorders. In the current context, television programmes can now be constructed from such videos (*Video Diary, You've been Framed*), which, while they may not measure up to overall broadcast standards, are still adequate for transmission.

Concerning analytical skills, another set of transitions can be identified. Consumers tend to use analytical skills in a relatively general manner, but, given the internalist nature of analytical skills, they will be using them less often than those located in the other continuum positions. Further, such judgements would tend to revolve around the relatively untheorized areas of taste, for example the hearing of a record on the radio which, in consumer mode, we say that we like. The fan tends to mobilize analytical skills within the genre or the corpus: 'This is a better record than Take That's last one', '*Coronation Street* is relatively boring at the moment', and so on. The cultist becomes immersed in comparisons within the genre and between shows themselves, and analytical skills become exceptionally developed. He or she will know when a character in a long-running show has knowledge which they could not possibly have within the show's world, but will also use such knowledge to deal with such 'problems'. As Jenkins (1992a) explains:

> *Star Trek* fans have found ways to explain away such apparent continuity problems as Khan's recognition of Chekov in *Star Trek: The Wrath of Khan* even though Chekov had not yet become a program regular when the Enterprise last crossed paths with Khan in 'Space Seed' or radical reworkings of the make-up for the Klingons between the television series and the feature films. The fans have come to accept that their ideal *Star Trek* never aligns perfectly with what producers provide. (p. 104)

Such skills are often used to develop the world of the show itself, in part forming the basis for the productive activity associated with cultists and enthusiasts. The immersion in the world of the text facilitates the development of the new texts. The immersion in the world of music facilitates the enthusiastic development of new texts as the rules of the genre become exceptionally clear. The enthusiast is less involved in comparison as he or she becomes immersed in the production within the network of the enthusiasm. The analytical skills are taken for granted. Interestingly, the generic and textual comparisons become more salient for the petty producer: as the place of the text within the marketplace of texts becomes salient, this leads into the examination of interpretative skills.

The consumer may make a number of interpretative comparisons. However, these are more likely to be in the referential mode (Liebes and Katz, 1993). Thus, *Coronation Street* will be compared with real life, or with other soap opera like *EastEnders*, especially along the plane of the extent to which they compare with the consumer's own experience. The issue of taste is again important, in particular as it will inform consumption decisions. Thus, within a context of relatively dispersed media use, for example the purchase of CDs, it is important to make judgements along the lines of 'Shall I purchase this CD rather than that one?' Essentially this is the basis for consumer choice. The fan becomes more focused on particular genres or types of text, making comparisons within the genre, but also mobilizes interpretative skills in the defence of the fan object from those who attack it. Real-life or referential functions have to do with fan identity rather than whether the text reflects experience or reality. The cultist develops greater analytical skills, and in the context of music may make extreme claims for the way in which the cult object reflects or organizes experience. Thus, cult followers of black rap will mobilize analytical skills to argue that such performers represent their community, and so on. The enthusiast again makes less comparison as she or he is within the world of the object itself. Defence of the text is less salient since assumptions of value are made, or use is within the context of the enthusiasm itself. Again, the petty producer is different: interpretative skills again become important in relation to the market. However, the point here is to place material within a market, that is, to produce: 'Will I be able to sell?' rather than 'What should I consume?' Hence, significantly, the producer and the consumer are operating on a similar terrain of commodity relations.

DIFFERENTIAL PRODUCTION

Fiske (1992) has argued that fans are semiotically, enunciatively and textually productive. By *semiotic productivity* Fiske means that activity which is characteristic of popular culture as a whole. According to Fiske, it 'consists of the making of meanings of social identity and of social experience from the semiotic resources of the cultural commodity' (p. 37). When we make commodities mean something for us we are engaging in semiotic productivity. When such meanings are communicated to others, *enunciative productivity* takes place. One of the most important vehicles for enunciation is talk. Thus, according to Fiske, the verbal communication to others of the meanings that we have made for ourselves is an important way in which fans can form communities. However, Fiske cites other non-verbal examples of enunciative productivity such as the wearing of colours by football fans, and the Madonna fans who, in dressing like their idol, 'were not only constructing for themselves more empowered identities than those normally available to young adolescent girls but were putting those meanings into social circulation' (p. 38).

The third category of production, *textual productivity,* entails the production of texts for circulation within the fan community itself. As was shown earlier in this chapter, a great deal of recent research on fans has drawn attention to the ways in which fans produce texts, such as stories, paintings, songs and videos about the characters from their favourite television shows (for example, Bacon-Smith, 1992; Jenkins, 1992a). Fans write stories which place the characters from different television shows in different contexts and allow the development of aspects of the original text to which fans feel attracted. This may involve placing the characters in different universes, or bringing characters from different shows together in one story. Fans also paint pictures of different characters. These activities are discussed at fan conventions and the texts circulate in the fan community. In this section we want to address this issue of textual productivity in more detail, again pulling out the differences across the positions in our continuum to establish the purchase of our approach on this topic (see Figure 5.5).

In general our argument is that textual production increases in importance as one moves across the continuum. However, simply

Consumers	Fans	Cultists	Enthusiasts	Petty producers
Little textual production, but are involved in 'textual production' in *talk*, e.g. 'Did you see *Coronation Street* last night? . . . I don't think that Curly should marry Raquel . . .' 'Discursive' 'Part of everyday life'	Production exists, but is *incorporated* into everyday life	Important activity, becomes *central* to the everyday life of a knowable community	Textual production is subordinated to *'material' production* within the knowable community	Textual and material production for the market – an imagined community

FIGURE 5.5   *Textual production*

to assert this point misses the qualitative differences between the different positions along the continuum. Consumers, as the label would suggest, are involved in little textual production in the specific sense outlined here. However, it is important to note that they are involved in textual production through talk, which can often create alternative texts, even if these are fleeting and not written down. Thus conversations which centre on the actions in a soap opera will often suggest alternative actions for the characters to those given to them by the script writers. This constructs an alternative text within discourse, even if it is not then turned into a product with a textual presence which can be circulated independently of its producer (see further, Harrington and Bielby, 1995, and below). Such imaginative discursive reconstructions are actually facilitated by the circulation of knowledge of the stars and future happenings in soap operas in the tabloid press. This increases the consumer knowledge which can lead to the generation of alternative storylines. However, in general for consumers textual production is discursive in the sense of involving talk and is woven into the fabric of everyday life.

Fans also incorporate textual production into their everyday lives but they actually produce something 'material' which can be passed on to others. Therefore when young children act as fans, characters from films and television series will be incorporated into the general playground games but will also be included in their drawings. However, it is important to note that the logic of these games and drawings is not generated from the texts which are being reinterpreted themselves, or only indirectly. Thus, the Terminator or Robocop may appear in the games and drawings of children who have never seen the films, though they may possess the toys which have been 'spun off' from series and films as merchandise. Fans' textual activities are material, but tend to be generated from within the pre-existing concerns of everyday life.

Cultism represent a further move. Here, the material production of texts becomes a central aspect of the cult activity. The *Star Trek* fans discussed above generate new texts of a variety of types on the basis of the characters and situations depicted in the television programmes and films. These texts are then circulated within the fan or, in our terms, cult community. This community is potentially *knowable*, in Raymond Williams' (1970) terms, even if not all the participants are actually known to those within the cult network.

For the enthusiast, production has become central. The enthusiasm tends to revolve around the production of things, from railway models to plays to second-hand dresses. There may be textual productivity as well, but this is subordinated to the material production. However, this production is still located within the enthusiasm itself. This is where enthusiasts are different from those petty producers who are moving from the realm of production on the request of members of an enthusiasm, to production for the market itself. Here, production, rather than being located within patterns of network sociation, begins to be increasingly directed towards an anonymous market, where the consumers of the goods can only be *imagined*. Production here is generative of other activity, rather than being located within it. This shift is important as it represents a clear shift in the identity of the producer, leading us to a consideration of the notion of identity in the different places of the continuum.

DIFFERENTIAL IDENTITIES

In this section we explore some of the relationships between identification and identity. Hall (1996) has maintained that the relationships between identification and identity are of critical importance in the study of contemporary culture. His argument attempts to revitalize debates about the relationship between the positions offered for identification by texts of different types and the adoption of such positions, however transitory, in the construction and reconstruction of identity and subjectivity. As he says:

> I use 'identity' to refer to the meeting point, the point of *suture*, between on the one hand the discourses and practices which attempt to 'interpellate', speak to us or hail us into place as the social subjects of particular discourses, and on the other hand, the processes which produce subjectivities, which construct as subjects which can

be 'spoken'. Identities are thus points of temporary attachment to the subject positions which discursive practices construct for us. (pp. 5–6)

Hall, therefore, attempts to locate the discussion of identification and identity within a broadly post-structuralist framework and does this at a relatively high level of abstraction. However, the sort of approach he recommends has been illustrated by more substantive discussion. An important examination of these processes in the context of cinema viewing is provided by Stacey (1994). We therefore use this work here further to substantiate and demonstrate the differences between the places on the continuum described earlier in this chapter.

In an analysis of female audience response to the cinema of the 1940s, carried out through the examination of audience letters and questionnaires, Stacey identifies three themes or discourses: escapism, identification and consumerism. She suggests that the cinema was escapist in a number of concrete ways in this period. For example, it was a ritualized 'night out' to the comfort and 'material pleasure' of the cinema. Moreover, the cinema provided a shared experience and a sense of belonging to an audience and provided an escape from the war. Finally, the cinema offered not only escape *from* some of the discomforts and anxieties of the everyday, but also an escape *to* American wealth as represented by the stars and their surroundings.

Stacey distinguishes between the forms of identification which take place in the main during the watching of a film that 'involve fantasies about the relationship between the identity of the star and the identity of the spectator' (p. 137), and those which occur outside the cinema. The latter involve 'practice as well as fantasy, in that spectators actually transform some aspect of their identity as a result of the relationship to their favourite star' (p. 137). We shall suggest that the move from the former to the latter may also involve the move from fan to cultist.

Stacey identifies five main types of 'cinematic identificatory practices' which occur during the course of cinema viewing: devotion, adoration, worship, transcendence and aspiration and inspiration. The first three of these are particularly focused on the construction of the star's image and their contents are relatively clear from the categorization itself. The latter particularly involve connexions between 'escapism and identification' (p. 145). Transcendence involves the breakdown of the boundary between self and the star as the audience member fantasizes about becoming the star and feeling the emotions of the star. Stacey suggests that this involves the movement of the audience member to the star and that consequently it is the star who is predominant. In the final category the emphasis falls on the audience member's identity and the desire to transform this dominates. Stacey's discussion of these categories therefore involves the move towards the position where the audience member's identity is itself being transformed and the relation to the star affects everyday practice outside of the cinema itself. This leads her to the second strand identified above.

Stacey distinguishes four main types of 'extra-cinematic identificatory practices' (p. 159), which take place outside of the cinema itself: pretending, resembling, imitating and copying. In the first, the audience members would pretend to be the star with whom they identified and play at visiting other stars in their Beverly Hills mansions, for example. The 'fan takes on the identity of the star in a temporary game of make-believe' (p. 161). These connexions were often facilitated by connexions of 'shared physical appearance' (p. 161) which are involved in the category of resemblance. This differs from imitation, where there is a conscious effort at transformation towards the star. This involves taking on an aspect of the star's identity. The final category of copying is similar to imitation, though Stacey distinguishes them by arguing that audiences imitate 'behaviour and activities' and copy 'appearances' (p. 167). These activities therefore involve relations of similarity and difference.

The media consumer is likely to have little identification with a star or a programme; it may be something that he or she watches as part of his or her everyday life. This is true in particular of television, where it has been argued that stars are relatively unimportant by comparison with personalities. Owing to the everyday nature of the experience, the television consumer does not engage in the characteristic features that are identified by

Stacey. The fan, however, does engage in such practices and the images connected to them may involve television as much as any other medium. Thus, in particular relation to a star, or a group as well in the case of pop fans, the fan is involved in relations of devotion, adoration and worship. These are relations which are often expressed in accounts of fan feelings (for example, Aizlewood, 1994). The processes of transcendence, aspiration, inspiration and pretending are important in facilitating the shift from fan to cultist. Thus, children, for example, are particularly likely to be involved in relations of pretending as fans. At the point of becoming a cultist there is the type of physical transformation that is involved in imitating and copying. Through this process the fan often becomes a part of a very loosely organized cult community. The following shows how, having dressed up in Bay City Roller clothes in a process of imitating and copying, a small group of girls became a much larger group:

> Our estate was where the bus route terminated, and as the empty bus pulled into the stop, the conductor looked genuinely nervous. We whooped in delight, swarming upstairs so we could hang our scarves out of the window, breaking into choruses of BCR songs. As the bus progressed along its torturous route into town, the excitement increased. At each stop, more and more girls piled on, all of them in uniform and in the same over-excited mood. I'd never talked to total strangers like this before. We discussed our favourite Rollers, admired each other's banners and scarves, and, every so often, someone would shout out and we'd all join in, at the top of our voices: 'B-A-Y, B-A-Y, B-A-Y C-I-T-Y, and an R-O double L E-R-S, Bay City Rollers are the best!' No one told us to shut up. No one would dare. There were too many of us. (Garratt, 1994, pp. 82–3)

For Garratt, this was a relatively transient experience in that her membership of this cult only took up a small period of her life. However, for some subcultists and fans of the *Star Trek* type it is far more likely to be a long-lasting and more all-encompassing part or way of life. The other aspects of enthusiasm and production are then built upon the construction of such fan and cult identities, though, of course, many fans will remain just that, not moving into the places at the right-hand end of the continuum.

Identification and the reconstitution of identity can then facilitate the exercise of skill and production discussed above.

CONCLUSION: IDENTITY AND EVERYDAY LIFE

It is important to emphasize the fluidity of such identity formation and reformation. This is particularly pertinent in adolescence and young adulthood (Fine, 1983), and, as has been noted above, many of the retrospective accounts written by fans start at the point of the early teens or late childhood and may even locate the beginnings of fandom in the break-up of previously existing social ties and structures. However, much recent writing in the context of the postmodernism debate has suggested that such fluidity of identity formulation and reformulation is an increasingly import- ant aspect of contemporary life (for example, Bauman, 1996). This means that fan activities may be increasingly important in the formation of adult identities as well. This argument has been developed substantively in the discussion of day-time soap opera fans in the United States by Harrington and Bielby (1995). They examine a different type of fan from that considered by Bacon- Smith (1992), Jenkins (1992a) and Penley (1992) in that these are not fans who engage in the productive generation of new texts in the concrete sense on the basis of their fan attachments; rather, they suggest, fan feelings and identifications are central in the productive construction of identity. Their approach is 'to question not just what fans *do* but who they *are*' (Harrington and Bielby, 1995, p. 7). In important respects this lack of 'concrete' production is related to the pleasure that fans find in the already existing texts. As Harrington and Bielby explain, 'It is *because* female consumers of women's texts – including soaps – find it easier to identify with and find pleasure in the primary narrative that they rarely produce derivative texts' (p. 21). Harrington and Bielby also argue that drawing distinctions within the audience or between categories of fans involves doing more than looking at activities, 'because becoming and being a fan involves parallel processes of activity engagement and identity management' (p. 41). Hence, for Harrington and Bielby, viewers, or those who we have preferred to categorize as consumers, 'have to negotiate a "hump factor" before they can become regular watchers' (p. 87). This often involves being introduced to and familiarized with the genre by a friend or family member and will depend on the availability of a significant amount of time. Hence, partly because of the derision to which soaps and their fans are subjected, involvement tends to take place within a supportive environment. The increasing identification with the soap and the identity of soap fan is difficult.

As has been argued by Grossberg (1992a, 1992b, see further Longhurst, 1995, pp. 233–5), the fan forms an affective link to an object of attachment. This is critical to Harrington and Bielby's examination of soap fans, where pleasure in the product is central. This may be an essentially private pleasure, or it may become more public through participation in fan lunches, correspondence, computer bulletin boards, and so on. This partly serves to generate a 'viewer/fan continuum' for Harrington and Bielby (1995, p. 113), which can be mapped onto the discussion above. Three factors are discussed to locate the audience members in the continuum: whether they are 'breadth' or 'depth' watchers who prefer a genre or are attached to one particular programme only; the 'position of access' or what it is about the soap that particularly engages the fan or viewer; and, finally, the nature of the particular show that they watch (pp 113–15). Harrington and Bielby emphasize the pleasure that is involved in these affective connexions and suggest that this should be considered in its own sense as a form of love attachment rather than being explained in other terms as a form of struggle and opposition.[7] In what in our terms is a clear distinction of IRP concerns from those of the SPP, they emphasize the play and pleasure that is involved in fandom. This does not mean that they ignore struggle and opposition, but as we have argued in general terms, they relocate these ideas in a different framework with an emphasis on spectacle and performativity. They argue:

> Unlike most media theorists who posit a barrier between subject and object, we believe that soap watching (like reading or fantasy gaming) is simultaneously a spectator and participant activity. It is participatory in that the story and the alternative world do not exist until we consciously and actively engage the text . . .; it is a spectator activity in

that we necessarily adopt a bordered position to the fictional world. (p. 132)

This difference is directly caught in Harrington and Bielby's conclusion, where they contrast their approach to the (IRP) line of Janice Radway:

Our suggestions may seem remarkably similar to Radway's conclusions concerning readers of romance novels, but they differ in an important way: we do not find soap fans' control over space to be fundamentally organized by ideological concerns, as Radway interprets romance readers' to be. Instead, soap fans' practices are guided by a sense of agency – an awareness of their ability as socially embedded individuals to initiate and control behaviour. . . . Soap fans' viewing choices and practices emerge for a myriad of reasons, including pleasure and experience of emotion. The concept of agency more adequately captures the general process of intentionality that is obscured by a focus on hegemonic resistance . . . what fans are or what they do are extensions of their integration and participation in viewing and everyday life. (pp. 178–9)

On the basis of our earlier consideration of general processes, we can suggest that the sorts of fan and enthusiast activities described, conceptualized and classified in this chapter are becoming increasingly prevalent in contemporary everyday life.[8] However, on this basis, how are these attachments and processes of production and consumption to be investigated? We shall address these issues in the next chapter.

NOTES

1. Of the twenty-eight fan accounts contained in the collections edited by Aizlewood (1994) and Roberts (1994), only four are written by women, and one of these is an updating of her connections to the Bay City Rollers by Garratt (1994). Aizlewood (1994) suggests two reasons for this gender imbalance: 'Firstly, being more mature than men, maybe women reach and discard their obsessions earlier. Secondly, music journalism is a macho thing and, shamefully, women aren't made welcome enough to see it through. Decide for yourself. I genuinely don't know' (p. xiv).
2. In this respect, and others, these accounts are part of the same phenomenon as the development, in Britain at least, of a new wave of men's 'style' or 'lifestyle' magazines, which are increasingly reliant upon what may be called 'soft-core'

pornographic images. Thus, the magazine *Loaded* promotes itself as the 'magazine for men who should know better'.

3. Whilst there are always dangers in reading fiction sociologically, some of these themes have been clearly explicated in Hornby's recent novel *High Fidelity* (1995). The narrative is in effect driven by the central male character's musings on his earliest relationships with women, re-capitulations of which have produced his lifelong inability to sustain a relationship, including his current one, which is breaking down. Likewise, his relations with his parents, who live in the far reaches of the north London suburbs, are problematic, partly because of their inability to grasp the hero's difficulties. This, of course, is partly narrated in the Hornby universe through characterizations of their own lack of taste – where they live, the films they watch, and so on.

4. Hence, even though Smith (1995) tries to become a pop star himself, and much of his book charts the ups and downs of this 'career', he still makes much of his fan attachments to a relatively small number of artists.

5. The example of Hornby's (1995) novel again springs to mind, where the central character's girl-friend explicitly condemns his inability to relate to anyone with a small and/or unhip record collection. See also Harrington and Bielby (1995) for some evidence for our general claim here.

6. As was classically realized by Karl Mannheim (1952).

7. It would be interesting to reconsider the accounts written by Wise (1990) and Garratt (1984, 1994) in this respect. Wise's use of Elvis as a teddy bear is especially informative in the context of Silverstone's (1994) and Harrington and Bielby's (1995) adoption of Winnicott's transitional object theory in the formulation of accounts of media identity and the role of television in everyday life.

8. Harrington and Bielby (1995, pp. 151–3), in a tantalizingly brief discussion, identify three social factors in the context of the generation of fan practices and identities: the increased space given to the airing of fan views in magazines, and so on, and the increased salience of celebrity magazines which provide information about stars' lives on which to construct fantasies and identifications (consider the success of *Hello* magazine in Britain, for example); technological advancement in the importance of computer contact between fans, and so on; and the decline of 'conventional' identifications around class, gender, and so on, which in previous times may have resulted in fan-like attachments and pleasures, and relatedly the increased importance and availability of forms of popular culture.

6

The Spectacle/Performance Paradigm: Methods, Issues and Theories

Our argument in this book has identified the emergence of a new paradigm in the study of the audience, which is itself related to the changing nature of the place of the media in the social life of the contemporary advanced Western world. We have argued that there are currently three types of audience: the simple, the mass and the diffused. The Spectacle/Performance paradigm that we have outlined concerns itself with the relationship between these different types of audience as they interact. It is worth repeating that the diffused audience has not replaced simple or mass audiences, which in some respects have become even more important than ever. It is possible to suggest, however, that the emergence of the diffused audience and the important interaction between spectacle, narcissism and performance has importantly changed the relationship between these different audience types and their content.

This can be considered through the example of contemporary football. The simple audience which attends the football match can become members of the mass audience when they watch a programme of edited highlights of the match they have attended after the game. Such highlights (or the full match itself) may then be recorded for repeat viewing and resources for discussion and the sort of fantasy and day-dreaming discussed in Chapter 4.

To point to other processes, the simple audience at a contemporary football match tends to dress in a particular fashion, with many audience members wearing team shirts and jackets displaying the team logo. This simple audience style, which has developed from the days when supporters would wear hats and scarves in team colours, is now of a vastly more significant scale and spills over into the performative diffused audience of everyday life where the wearing of football shirts has become a day-to-day activity. Interestingly, in relation to the performative nature of tourism and the idea of spectacle discussed in Chapter 3, such display is particularly significant on tourist holidays abroad as a very visible signifier of a form of identity. The shirts of many European teams are worn in this way. Moreover, workers in tourist destinations would be familiar with the shirts and logos of many different teams (and perhaps possess them) through the mass audience activity of watching football on television and by interaction in and with the diffused audience of the everyday life of the resort. Thus, in important ways, the local and the global are brought together and re-patterned in particular locales to produce new forms of the universalism of the diffused audience. We shall have more to say about these processes in the conclusion to this chapter.

One important issue to consider following this, therefore, is the ways in which these increasingly complex interactions in everyday life and between different audience forms can be studied sociologically. Our argument is that neither the methods of the BP nor those of the IRP can hope to capture this complexity. The BP has tended to use survey or structured interview data to evaluate the effects of media exposure upon the audience members, or to use self-report studies to consider the gratifications which the media function to fulfil through use. The media message was often considered as a stimulus in this sort of approach (Livingstone, 1990). The IRP expressly critiqued these methods. Two main stands were developed. First, the study of the text was itself prioritized and was carried out with the increasingly sophisticated methods of structuralism and semiotics. In part this facilitated and expanded the conception of the media message as a text itself. Second, the preferred method for the study of the audience was the focus group, used at different levels of sophistication. Despite the claims of the paradigm to ethnographic methods, it has long been accepted even by some of its advocates that its methods could not be termed properly ethnographic in any sense that would be recognized by anthropological writers. This has tended to lead the paradigm to a proliferation of focus group studies, which may have been beneficial in that they have opened up empirical consideration of audiences rather than theoretical speculation, but which do not adequately capture the complexity of contemporary audience activity. The research that has tended to move knowledge forward has actually shifted to a much more ethnographic stance where the audience is much more securely located in the complex patterns and rhythms of contemporary everyday life (for example, Gillespie, 1995; Hermes, 1995). It is this approach that we suggest points the way forward for research within the SPP. This does not rule out focus group discussions, surveys or interviews, but recognizes that these can only be used adequately once they have been contextualized in everyday life, that is, once they have been relocated in an alternative place in a different paradigm. Moreover, it does not rule out the semiotic analysis of texts, but again maintains that such analyses are potentially very unhelpful if they are not further related to the place of the text in everyday life (Hermes, 1995).[1]

Consequently, in the first part of this chapter we offer some pointers to our view of the preferred methodology for the study of the contemporary audience. This discussion generates a consideration of some key sociological issues: the form of current identity formation; the nature of trust and social capital; and the relationship between contemporary social integration and disintegration. In examining these issues we are concerned to connect our extended discussion of the nature of audiences to some matters of contemporary social and sociological significance. The fact that we see our analysis as leading in this direction should come as no surprise, given the emphasis that we have already placed upon the centrality of the diffused audience to social life.

SCENES AND LOCALITIES

Our suggestion is that the investigation into the nature of the diffused audience should start with particular specific localities. One area where this sort of approach has become increasingly important is in studies of contemporary music production and consumption. The most comprehensive study of local music-making to date was undertaken by the anthropologist Ruth Finnegan (1989) between 1980 and 1984 in the English new town of Milton Keynes. Finnegan examines seven musical worlds: classical, brass band, folk, musical theatre, jazz, country and western, and rock and pop. She draws a series of contrasts between the overlapping worlds in terms of how the playing of music is learned, how it is performed and how it is written. She identifies a number of different social institutions which support music and the patterns of organization of the musical worlds, and, in general, points to the importance of music to everyday life in Milton Keynes in providing pathways for urban living. Finnegan's detailed empirical study suggests that music is a core activity in the structuring of contemporary social life: an argument which has been made in far more theoretical terms by writers like John Shepherd (for example, 1991) and Tia de Nora (1995). Moreover, in *The Hidden Musicians* Finnegan (1989) explores the often drawn distinction between professional and amateur musicians. However, she argues that the distinction between amateur and professional is in practice very difficult to draw:

> The term 'professional' . . . at first appears unambiguous. A 'professional' musician earns his or her living by working full time in some musical role, in contrast to the 'amateur', who does it 'for love' and whose source of livelihood lies elsewhere. But complications arise as soon as one tries to apply this to actual cases on the ground. Some lie in ambiguities in the concept of 'earning one's living', others in differing interpretations about what is meant by working in 'music', and others again – perhaps the most powerful of all – in the emotive overtones of the term 'professional' as used by the participants themselves. (p. 13).

Therefore, Finnegan argues that the relationship between amateur and professional can best be seen as a continuum, and most of the musicians playing in Milton Keynes can be seen as working at some points in the middle of a continuum of the type identified and discussed in the previous chapter. In many respects the key term used to describe the musicians studied by Finnegan is 'performer'. Thus, Finnegan argues that her research leads me further to query once again not only the still fashionable view that human beings somehow gain their central social reality from their *economic* involvement in society (usually based on the 'man as paid worker' model) but even the richer and, in my opinion, more realistic 'man as symboliser' approach (current in some social science, specially anthropology), with its overtones of an ideational and ultimately linguistically modelled view of humanity. It is surely equally valid to picture human beings essentially as practitioners and performers: artistic and moral enactors rather than as symbolic perceivers or paid workers. (p. 341)

It is important to take all these different dimensions into account in considering the activities of fans and the complex sets of relationships between producers and consumers, production and consumption in the contemporary diffused audience. In accord with the suggestions of Finnegan, and as we have shown in Chapter 5, those relations should be seen as continua.

The approach adopted by Finnegan points the way forward for contemporary audience research. Three aspects of this are critical. First, there is the already emphasized ethnographic dimension. Finnegan's study reports on detailed fieldwork carried out over a significant period of time. In many respects the investments, especially in the time expended in research, are huge. However, the pay-offs are important, as she provides a clear and sophisticated picture of this area of music production and audience activity. Second, Finnegan points to the way in which music is used to structure 'pathways' of life. Music, then, is not something which is conceived in terms of its effects or how it is used; moreover, its ideological role in the maintenance of hegemonic activities is not emphasized. Rather, it is part and parcel of the threads of day-to-day living and interaction. Third, there is Finnegan's emphasis on the performative nature of music-making, which leads her in the passage cited above to offer a new philosophical anthropology which emphasizes the performative nature of human beings in general. It is the generality of the claim made here about the performativity of the interconnexions of the audience to the media which we take to be of crucial significance. Some more recent work has attempted to theorize these relations further, especially in relation to the performative dimensions of musical activity. Of particular importance here has been the development of the concept of the scene.

Straw (1991) draws on the earlier work of Barry Shank to define the musical scene as distinct from the older notion of the musical community as

> that cultural space in which a range of musical practices coexist, interacting with each other within a variety of processes of differentiation, and according to widely varying trajectories of change and cross-fertilization. The sense of purpose articulated within a musical community normally depends on an affective link between two terms: contemporary musical practices, on the one hand, and the musical heritage which is seen to render this contemporary activity appropriate to a given context, on the other. Within a music scene, that same sense of purpose is articulated within those forms of communication through which the building of musical alliances and the drawing of musical boundaries take place. The manner in which musical practices within a scene tie themselves to processes of historical change occurring within a larger international musical culture will also be a significant basis of the way in which such forms are positioned within that scene at a local level. (p. 373)

The development and operationalization of the concept of the scene has been carried forward in Barry Shank's *Dissonant Identities* (1994). On one level, Shank charts the changing nature of the music scene in Austin, Texas. This, though significant, is not of primary concern here. Rather, we want to emphasize Shank's more theoretical consideration of the idea of scene, which he defines 'as an overproductive signifying community; that is, far more semiotic information is produced than can be rationally parsed' (p. 122). Moreover, 'The constitutive feature of local scenes of live musical performance is their evident display of semiotic disruption, their potentially dangerous overproduction and exchange of musicalized signs of identity and community' (p. 122). It is important that within scenes conventional divisions between producers and consumers become blurred, thus 'within this fluid stream of potential meanings, the audience and the musicians together participate in a nonverbal dialogue about the significance of the music and the construction of their selves (p. 125). Most importantly for our general discussion:

Spectators become fans, fans become musicians, musicians are always already fans, all constructing the nonobjects of identification through their performances as subjects of enunciation – becoming and disseminating the subject-in-process of the signifying practice of rock 'n' roll music. (p. 131)

Of course, Shank constructs this argument around the particular medium of rock in a designated place and Straw is concerned with musical scenes. However, it seems obvious that a clear distinction between musical and other forms of production and consumption cannot be sustained. The advent and success of music videos and music television is but one clear indicator of this. Cultural production increasingly takes place across different media, which are promoted intertextually (see, for example, Negus, 1996, pp. 66–96). Audiences, as we have already argued, also increasingly roam across and between different media. Therefore, it can be suggested that those processes of identification and the production of self in a spectacularized society increasingly involve the interactions of different media.

Further evidence for these points can be found in a discussion of the development of rock and roll in Memphis (Gordon, 1995). In his attempt to consider those aspects of the Memphis scene not normally addressed by historians of rock and roll, Gordon includes as culturally significant the examples of a wrestler (Sput-nick Monroe) and a film Western hero (Lash Laruo). Moreover, Gordon, in accord with other cultural historians of Memphis rock (for example, Guralnick 1995), emphasizes the place of Dewey Phillips' radio show, where Elvis's first Sun single was premiered. However, what was important was not simply the music that was played, but also the way it was contextualized and located within the frame of the radio show and the personality of the presenter. In important respects the Memphis scene might be thought to have been at the cutting edge of late modernity in the early 1950s. Patterns of interaction were being developed which would later become commonplace, with different mass media interacting in a particular location in what was at that point the most media-saturated society in the world. It is also important to note how these developments relied on media-facilitated interactions between different social groups, so that Elvis could hear 'black' music and blacks could hear his. This is not to say that this was the only place where this was happening in the US, but that it is perhaps the most clearly documented so far.

In general our argument is that this concept of scene, initially developed in the study of popular music, is potentially useful in the analysis of the patterns of sociation of members of the diffused audience. In any scene, there are likely to be a number of interacting media in the production of spaces from which to develop the kinds of intensity of attachment and perhaps subsequent production of textual forms that we have described in some detail in the previous chapter. One important point to emphasize is the extraordinary complexity of those interactions.

What might this mean for the sociological investigation of the contemporary diffused audience? First, we suggest that it is important to get as close to the everyday life of participants in the diffused audience as possible. Participants will need to be interviewed and to be observed in the activities of daily life. Interaction and activities within households are important here, but they can only be properly evaluated from within the wider process of identification of networks and patterns. Interviews in the home can be a starting point, but it is important to recognize that this is all that they can be. Likewise, there is nothing wrong with the utilization of data produced by survey methods, provided that it is located in the understanding of the everyday. Such research suggests that while there are clear differences in the patterns of consumption of media, these can only be properly understood within a fuller understanding of the everyday life of the audience. However, it also means considering the meaning of everyday life itself. We have already distanced our conception of performativity from that associated with interactionist sociologists such as Goffman (see Chapter 3), and it is important to stress that our conception of the everyday is likewise built upon developments which argue for the contemporary centrality of the media in sociation. This has been a significant move made in cultural studies and accounts of the media audience in recent years. Thus, Drotner (1994) has also shown how the development of more qualitative and ethnographic work on the media audience has led to a stress on the idea of everyday life. She argues that 'To date, no media ethnographer has defined what he or she means by this concept' (p. 346), and attempts to rectify this omission. She identifies pessimistic (in the work of Lefebvre) and optimistic (in de Certeau) theorizations of everyday life. The importance of Lefebvre, in her view, is that

> he makes a crucial connection between modernity and the development of the everyday, and he emphasizes that the everyday infuses all aspects of life, not merely the family or leisure. These aspects are timely reminders also to scholars of media reception who all too often fail to situate their investigations in a specific historical perspective, and whose emphasis on one mass medium tends to obscure the influence of other media. (p. 348)

Drotner suggests that Lefebvre's follower de Certeau is far more optimistic in his approach to contemporary everyday life, but that he tends to idealize resistance in everyday life and overplays the carnivalesque (p. 349). In important respects de Certeau can be located within the PP, as detailed earlier. This more celebratory approach has been criticized by Grossberg (1992a), who offers a distinction between everyday life and daily life. Broadly, everyday life is the province of the 'better-off' (the majority of the population of the advanced capitalist societies of the West). Everyday life is also routinized and mundane:

> there is a real pleasure and comfort in its mundanity, in the stability of its repetitiveness. Not only its practices but also its investments are routinized. In a sense, one need never worry about living within the maps of everyday life. Instead, one gets to 'choose' how one instantiate the maps, what matters, where one invests. In everyday life, one has the luxury of investing in the mundane and the trivial, in the consumption of life itself. To offer the simplest example, there is a real security and pleasure in knowing when and where and exactly for what (including brands) one will go shopping next. (p. 149)

Grossberg distinguishes 'everyday life' from the 'daily life' of those whose do not possess the economic, political and social resources to generate an everyday life. He uses the example of the place of rap music among blacks in the contemporary US. Rap, in his view, addresses the concerns of those who are excluded from everyday life and constantly emphasizes political and economic matters. Moreover, the everyday life of the better-off is renewed and 'spiced up' by the appropriation of forms from others' daily lives – a constant cycle in the appropriation of various forms of music.

Grossberg thus tends to move the idea of everyday life away from concepts of opposition and resistance in a way similar to that derived from Schütz by Drotner (1994, p. 350). In our terms, this signals a move from the IRP to the SPP. Likewise, Drotner attempts to break with the notion of the everyday as resistant through adapting two terms from Schütz: repetition and recognition. Thus everyday life is both repetitive in its established patterns (as in Grossberg) and based on the recognition of texts and the giving of meaning to them. This current work, then, has removed the idea of everyday life from within the domain concerns of the IRP.

The implication of this move is that research has to be centrally concerned with the mapping of the activities of the everyday life of the diffused audience. Jameson (1988) has pointed out that one way forward for the social sciences is in the 'cognitive mapping' of cultural practices. The key problem with this is that it over-rationalizes, in the name of a form of Marxist ideology-critique, the processes of contemporary everyday life, and would not take into account the development of the concept of everyday life as considered above.[2] Empirical research into audiences at heritage sites and museums has pointed rather to the role of the emotions in the understanding and mapping of audience members, leading Bagnall (1996) to argue for the significance of the role of 'emotional mapping'. Bagnall shows how three different kinds of mapping interact in the consumption of heritage sites. First, the sites are mapped physically by visitors in that they move around the site in a very direct way. This form of mapping also locates the bodily dimension of this form of audience activity. Museums and heritage sites increasingly engage the senses in a variety of different ways. This physical and bodily mapping forms the base on which other forms of mapping take place. It can be suggested that this form of physical or bodily mapping applies to the contemporary mediascape where the diffused audience is at work as well. Indeed the heritage sites analysed by Bagnall are a significant part of that mediascape. However, it is often forgotten that activities that involve interaction with media are intensely physical activities. Television 'relaxation' does not occur in the same way without some kind of comfortable chair to ease back into. Music is an intensely physical activity. The relationship between music and dance and movement is obvious. However, music is part of the physical fabric in perhaps other less obvious but critical ways as well. As one of the respondents in the 'Music in Daily Life' project put it (see Chapter 2): 'Music is just part of life, like air. You live with it all the time, so it's tough to judge what it means to you' (Crafts et al., 1993, p. 109).

Emotional mapping can take two forms: confirmatory or rejective. In the confirmatory mode, the heritage sites studied by Bagnall engaged the emotions of their visitors, who then felt that they were emotionally connected to something that was 'real' or at least plausible. However, for example, personal memories can sometimes lead to the rejection of the picture presented by the museum. This emotional engagement can then in some cases lead to the development of more 'reasoned' rejections of the museum exhibits.

Third, Bagnall points to the connexion between this mode of emotion and the role of the imagination. We have already identified the importance of Campbell's arguments in this respect (see Chapter 4). As Bagnall (1996) argues:

> it is easier to imagine events or situations which produce an emotion in the imaginer. Nostalgia is an appropriate emotion for it is largely self-referential. Thus, the sites at Wigan [Pier] and Manchester [Museum of Science and Industry] can successfully utilize nostalgia and the emotions it generates as a means to stimulate the imagination. Moreover, individuals now have a greater capacity for imagining because they are continuously bombarded with images and, frequently, images from the past. (p. 239)

In this sense we can see how the emotions and imagination are engaged in a crucial way in audiencing activity. Our hypothesis is that this is a specific instance of a general pattern. Another way to consider this process is to use the idea of plotting (Somers, 1994; see further Longhurst and Savage, 1996).

Second, it is critically important to consider the relationships of different forms of media to the everyday life of participants. The discussion of scenes and local music production and consumption has pointed to the interaction of different media within contemporary local environments. Methodologies which focus on single media and/or particular types of text seem singularly inappropriate to the understanding and mapping of the contemporary mediascape, even as a starting point. Thus, what is important is not just the patterns of the everyday life of the diffused audience as they go about their day-to-day activities (sometimes becoming members of simple and mass audiences), but the mapping of the mediascape to which they relate in that everyday life. That mediascape is increasingly complex and global, and raises a number of issues which have become increasingly prevalent. Let us begin with the first of these which has already been discussed at several points in this book so far.

IDENTITY

Simon Frith (1996) has argued that 'Music constructs our sense of identity through the direct experiences it offers of the body, time and sociability, experiences which enable us to place ourselves in imaginative cultural narratives. Such a fusion of imaginative fantasy and bodily practice marks also the integration of aesthetics and ethics' (p. 124). In making this argument, Frith criticizes those accounts of music which point to its essentially representational role. Music rather is constructive in that 'it creates and constructs an experience' (p. 109). For Frith, music is a 'key to identity because it offers, so intensely, a sense of both self and others, of the subjective in the collective' (p. 110). Moreover,

> what makes music special – what makes it special for identity – is that it defines a space without boundaries (a game without frontiers). Music is thus the cultural form best able to cross borders – sounds carry across fences and walls and oceans, across classes, races and nations – and to define places; in clubs, scenes, and raves, listening on headphones, radio and in the concert hall, we are only where the music takes us. (p. 125)

While there is no denying the place that music plays in such constructions of identity (see further Grossberg, 1992b), it is not clear that music alone plays such a role. Therefore, it can be argued, first, that there is no reason why other media and activities should not play an equal or greater role for the construction of some individuals' identities, and, second, that again the interaction of different media in the construction of identity needs to be emphasized. In part this is linked to technological innovation, in that television, for example, can now cross boundaries much more easily because of satellites, but it is also due to the wide distribution of particularly popular American television programmes, which, as Liebes and Katz (1993) have shown for the example of *Dallas* and Gripsrud (1995) has demonstrated for *Dynasty*, can be interacted with in different contexts on a global scale. Consider also the global distribution of *Star Trek* and its central role in the construction of identities for the fans discussed in the previous chapter. Further, music does not always exist in isolation from other important global media. As we have already emphasized, there is the important example of music video, which brings together visual image and music. However, despite these points, which suggest that the roles of different media are actually rather more important than Frith concedes, it is possible to concur with his emphasis that 'Identity is thus necessarily a matter of ritual, it describes one's place in a dramatized pattern of relationships' (Frith, 1996, p. 125), and to suggest that the complex interactions of the diffused audience are critical in constructions of contemporary identities. However, while we have concurred with this emphasis on identity, it is important to reconnect this to some of the ideas about locality and scene we have made above. In this respect, Grossberg (1996) has made some suggestive comments.

In a critique of the recent centrality of ideas of identity in cultural studies, Grossberg (1996) argues that much debate in this area has remained on the plane of 'modern logic', which operates on the terrain of modern power. This modern logic is constituted around 'difference, individuality, and temporality' (p. 93). Grossberg argues that this framework reproduces identities which are fragmentary rather than those which can foster new senses of inclusion. He is critical of Derridean notions of difference and argues instead for a particular version of Foucault's theory and concept of power. Arguing for a consideration of identity based on otherness rather than the linguistically situated relational concept of difference, he concerns himself with the concreteness of constructions of self and community. Identities, then, are not simply defined in relation to other identities within discourse. Most importantly for our current purposes, Grossberg emphasizes space and place over temporality and argues that identity needs to be rethought in spatial terms. For Grossberg, this reintroduces a notion of community, 'where community defines an abode marking people's ways of belonging within the structured mobilities of contemporary life' (p. 105).

The arguments we have advanced in the previous section of this chapter concerning the need to map and to plot the scenes and locales of the diffused audience chime with this spatial conceptualization of identity. However, we would again emphasize, in a way that Grossberg does not in the paper we have just cited, that role of contemporary media in this scenic construction of identity within the diffused audience. Moreover, this emphasis on community raises important issues concerning the meaning of contemporary community in an increasingly marketized, commodified and media-saturated society. In particular, it points to issues of trust, inclusion and exclusion.

TRUST, INCLUSION AND EXCLUSION

In his synthesizing work on the nature of modernity in the early 1990s, Giddens (1990, 1991) identified the centrality of trust in contemporary, late modern societies. He defined trust as 'confidence in the reliability of a person or system, regarding a given set of outcomes or events, where that confidence expresses a faith in the probity or love of another, or in the correctness of abstract principles (technical knowledge)' (Giddens, 1990, p. 34). He pointed importantly to the role for trust in the maintenance of what he termed the 'extended time–space distanciation associated with modernity' (p. 87). Giddens in a number of places suggests the centrality of the mass media of communication in the relations of trust and modernity. These comments are taken up by Silverstone (1994) in his path-breaking work *Television and Everyday Life*. Drawing on Winnicott as well as Giddens, Silverstone points to the centrality and taken-for-granted nature of television in contemporary everyday life, as well as its importance in the maintenance of trust relations. Within the genres of television, it is news which, in Silverstone's view, is central here. As he argues, 'it is the news, I think, which holds pride of place as the genre in which it is possible to see most clearly the dialectical articulation of anxiety and security – and the creation of trust – which overdetermines television as a transitional object, particularly for adult viewers' (p. 16). We shall want to develop this approach below, by broadening out this point of view to consider the interaction of media in the mediascape of the diffused audience, rather than focusing on television alone. We shall develop this argument via the work of Fukuyama (1995).

Fukuyama (1995) describes his work as offering a corrective to the narrow focus of classical economics, in that he argues that cultural factors are of crucial significance in the creation of wealth and in the different economic performances of nation-states. In particular, the extent and nature of trust relationships is paramount in such relationships. Thus, societies which are high in 'social capital', which is 'a capability that arises from the prevalence of trust in a society or in certain parts of it' (p. 26), are high in economic capital and wealth also. Fukuyama makes some divisions in social capital. In particular he suggests that 'The most useful kind of social capital is often not the ability to work under the authority of a traditional community or group, but the capacity to form new associations and to cooperate within the terms of reference they establish' (p. 27).

In developing his arguments concerning economic performance, culture, trust and social capital, Fukuyama places particular stress on the nature of family structure and interaction, especially in the growth of firms and businesses. This is a rather narrow operationalization and indication of the nature of culture, as Fukuyama recognizes in a number of rather brief asides where he points to the significance of the formation of 'spontaneous sociability' (p. 26). We do not want to deny the significance of the family and family interaction, but rather to suggest that the increased and increasing interaction of the members of the diffused audience with each other and a variety of media is likely to be significant in the generation of trust and patterns of inclusion and exclusion, with all that suggests for notions of well-being. This is also likely to be the case in societies, like Britain, where there is rapid formation and reformation of families. Developing Silverstone's arguments concerning the role of television as a transitional object in child development, it is possible to argue that media are increasingly the lubricant for the passage from one family structure to another. We constructed a similar idea from a rather different route in the previous chapter when we considered the place of fan attachments and activities in the transition to adulthood and the break-up of the fan's family. We are now in a position to suggest some links between this strand of our argument which pointed to distinction within the diffused audience and these larger issues being addressed in this section.

We can suggest at the very least that all the accounts of trust examined so far in this section actually underplay the significance of media and audience activities in their accounts of interaction and social processes. This is despite the fact that Giddens offers a suggestive general account, Silverstone very significantly develops Giddens and points to the centrality of television in trust and personality formation, and Fukuyama graphically demonstrates the significance of social capital, trust and performance as related to culture as exemplified by the family. Our point is that it is impossible to understand the nature of social interaction without understanding the role of audiencing. Some evidence for these suspicions can be found in some recent work on middle-class and managerial culture.

In part this theme is based in a critique of Bourdieu's approach, which associates a distinct pattern of cultural taste with classes and sections of classes. Recent American literature has pointed to the fact that rather than having a set of 'snobbish' or highbrow tastes, middle-class people are increasingly omnivorous and eclectic in cultural terms (Peterson and Kern, 1996; Peterson and Simkus, 1992). The finding here is that 'Not only are high-status Americans far more likely than others to consume the fine arts but . . . they are also more likely to be involved in a wide range of low-status activities' (Peterson and Kern, 1996, p. 900). However, there is not a simple attachment to 'low-status activities' but a structure which suggests that some are far more likely to be consumed by the middle classes than others. Patterns in these forms of association have been identified, where it has been suggested that cultural tolerance should not be conceptualized as an indiscriminate tendency to be nonexclusive, but as a reordering of group boundaries that trades race for class' (Bryson, 1996, p. 895). Erickson (1996) points to the significance of 'sports' discussion as a facilitator of conversation and interaction in everyday exchanges in the security firms that she studied in Canada. Our suggestion is that these developing patterns of taste and interaction which point to increased fluidity in taste are connected to the rise of the diffused audience and the patterns of distinction and classification within it. Moreover, to echo Fukuyama, in the words of Peterson and Kern (1996): 'As highbrow snobbishness fits the needs of the earlier entrepreneurial upper-middle class, there also seems to be an elective affinity between today's new business-administrative class and omnivorousness' (p. 906). Thus, new patterns of trust and interaction seem to be developing which have potential implications for the generation of wealth and the relationships on which these processes rest. Therefore it seems that new patterns of inclusion and exclusion are developing. In the final section of this chapter we link this to the notion of the diffused audience more directly.

SOCIATION AND THE DIFFUSED AUDIENCE

In our earlier discussion of the diffused audience we argued for the significance of four interrelated dimensions. First, a large amount of time in contemporary Western societies is spent in consuming media of different types; we live in a 'media-drenched' society. Second, we have argued that the media are constitutive of everyday life. Third, we live in a performative society where, fourth, the world is spectacular and individuals are increasingly narcissistic. Our suggestion at the end of the previous section was that new patterns of everyday life can be understood via this notion of the diffused audience.

We have already mentioned briefly the argument of Bonnie Erickson concerning sports talk as a facilitator of interaction in cross-class situations. Erickson develops a critique of Bourdieu for his neglect of social capital, which, after introducing it in *Distinction* (1984), he then, in Erickson's (1996, p. 218) view neglects. This means that he tends not to pay enough attention to the actual complexity of networks of interaction. Within these networks of interaction, Erickson argues that 'the most widely useful form of cultural resource is *cultural variety* plus the (equally cultural) understanding of the rules of relevance' (p. 219). Erickson's important finding in this respect is that 'sports is a cross-class coordinating genre, popular in all class levels and widely seen as something in common with others at work' (p. 223). We can develop this finding in the context of the arguments we have been advancing in this book, using football as the audience activity that best represents sport in a British context.

If we are correct about the amount of time that is spent consuming media and the extent to which media are constitutive of everyday life, we would expect prominent issues within the media to be increasingly significant within everyday life, especially in the workplace where different groups are interacting. It can at the least be hypothesized that this is the case for football in contemporary Britain. Despite the arguments that are often advanced that the concentration of ownership and control will restrict access to cultural phenomena, there is currently more football available on British television than has ever been the case. This is especially true for those who subscribe to cable and satellite TV, but is still true even for those who have only terrestrial TV. This is not always live, but it is certainly possible with only a minimum amount of effort to see every goal scored by every team in the Premier League in every match in the season; likewise it is possible for all those with a TV and licence to see all the goals in the later stages of the FA cup. Fans, cultists and enthusiasts can compile their home videos of all their teams' goals at relatively low cost. The availability of this information facilitates interaction and discussion of football in everyday life. The raw materials for debate are available to the mass television audience and this discussion takes place in the diffused audience of everyday life, where sports talk is so significant.[3]

In this sense, the media are central to this development. This is also facilitated by the expansion of coverage of football in the daily press, where sports can take up a significant proportion of all newspapers (there is not a specialist football paper in Britain) and where even the 'quality' papers now have specialist sport supplements. Sport and sports news are central to a national radio channel and there is a number of mass circulation magazines aimed at an adult sports audience. The mass audience is increasingly addressed. These developments provide the context in which the more specific diffused audience processes can occur. Thus, in terms of performativity, a key use of this mass audience resource is for the performance and exercise of knowledge to gain forms of distinction.

These performances are not simply based around knowledge about the role of tactics, the skills of the players and the capabilities of managers, but also mobilize emotional mapping, in the sense identified by Bagnall (1996). Thus, these arguments develop increasing force when the emotions are engaged, as they almost immediately are in that most football talk is based in some intensity of attachment to a particular team or teams. Analytical performance is intrinsically related to emotional attachment. This emotional attachment is displayed in dress, in the wearing of team colours and logos in everyday life including workplaces, where players and teams will be displayed. Performances are constructive of individual selves and speed up the spectacularization of the world as described in earlier chapters. To fuel these processes there is, then, an increased desire for knowledge of different kinds leading to the demand for more information from the media. These processes can then form the kind of cycle represented in Figure 6.1.

Thus as we began this chapter by looking at the processes of the connections between the simple, the mass and the diffused audience using the example of football, so can we conclude in the same way. The availability of information to the mass audience, combined with the general processes we have outlined in the previous

FIGURE 6.1   *Contemporary football and the diffused audience*

chapters, allows the development of a particular sector of the diffused audience, where the resources are provided by football, which may lead to the increased salience of the simple audience, as people attend live matches. These processes allow the development of new and changing identities, and patterns of inclusion and exclusion based on knowledge and performance connected to the activity. Trust might be established on this basis, where little might otherwise exist. Thus, in addition to the much publicized rivalry between fans there is also the less commented on trust and interaction between fellow football fans, most of whom know that their team in the long run is not likely to be consistently successful. However, all these processes can interact to produce changes, for example in simple audience behaviour, where at the time of writing there have been complaints that members of the simple audience at football matches have moved from being fans or the cultists described in the previous chapter to being more like consumers who are waiting to be entertained.

This example is suggestive of the new complex patterns of interaction which characterize the contemporary audience. Our argument in this book has been that this complexity cannot fully be understood from within the BP or the IRP. The emergent paradigm which we have labelled the SPP is more able so to do. This is because it recognizes much more explicitly the 'media saturation' of everyday life and the consequent significance of performance, spectacle, narcissism and imagination. Moreover it re-conceptualizes the new patterns of media consumption and the role of fan and enthusiast activities.

Many of our arguments are speculative, though we have pointed to studies which we think support the general case made in the book. However, we do believe that much more research is needed on the topics and approach we have emphasized. Some ways forward have been offered in this chapter. We suggest therefore that research should begin from localities, that it should attempt to characterize the networks of everyday life and determine the audience nature of those networks. Such research may lead to the qualification of some of the general and particular claims of the book. However, that is the nature of 'normal' science within a paradigm.

NOTES

1. Hermes (1995) illustrates very clearly the problems with a semiotic or ideology critique approach to the study of women's magazines. Consider also the problems of semiotic deconstructions of contemporary advertising, when advertising is itself turning in on such deconstructions and using them, and where play and discussion of ads is itself an important lubricant of everyday life, particularly amongst young people (Willis, 1990)
2. In this respect it is interesting to note the approach taken to the Disney phenomenon by the group based at Duke University (Project on Disney 1995), where everyday practices are recurrently mapped onto a critique of the Disney phenomenon, which plays down that which is actually happening within the diffused audience of Disneyworld.
3. We could develop a similar argument for soap opera talk.
4. See Thornton (1995) for this process in youth subcultures around dance.

References

Abercrombie, N. (1980) *Class, Structure, and Knowledge*, Oxford: Blackwell.

Abercrombie, N. (1996) *Television and Society*, Cambridge: Polity.

Abercrombie, N., Hill, S. and Turner, B.S. (1980) *The Dominant Ideology Thesis*, London: Allen & Unwin.

Adorno, T.W. (1990) 'On Popular Music', in S. Frith and A. Goodwin (eds), *On Record: Rock, Pop, and the Written Word*, London: Routledge.

Adorno, T.W. (1993) 'A Social Critique of Radio Music', in N. Strauss (ed.), *Radiotext(e)*, New York: Semiotext(e). Issue 16, 6, 1 of *Semiotext(e)*.

Aizlewood, J. (ed.) (1994) *Love is the Drug*, London: Penguin.

Alloway, L. (1992) 'The Arts and the Mass Media', in C. Harrison and P. Wood (eds), *Art in Theory 1900–1990*, Oxford: Blackwell, pp. 700–3.

Anderson, B. (1991) *Imagined Communities: Reflections on the Origins and Spread of Nationalism* (revised edition), London: Verso.

Ang, I. (1989) 'Wanted: Audiences. On the Politics of Empirical Audience Studies', in E. Seiter, H. Borchers, G. Kreutzner and E.-M. Warth (eds), *Remote Control: Television Audiences and Cultural Power*, London: Routledge.

Appadurai, A. (1986), 'Introduction: Commodities and the Politics of Value', in A. Appadurai (ed.), *The Social Life of Things*, Cambridge: Cambridge University Press.

Appadurai, A. (1993) 'Disjuncture and Difference in the Global Cultural Economy', in B. Robins (ed.), *The Phantom Public Sphere*, Minneapolis and London: University of Minnesota Press.

Atkinson, J.M. (1984) *Our Masters' Voices*, London: Methuen.

Bacon-Smith, C. (1992) *Enterprising Women: Television Fandom and the Creation of Popular Myth*, Philadelphia: University of Pennsylvania Press.

Bagnall, G. (1996) 'Consuming the Past', in S. Edgell, K. Hetherington and A. Warde (eds), *Consumption Matters*, Oxford: Blackwell/Sociological Review.

Baldwin, E., Longhurst, B., McCracken, S., Ogborn, M. and Smith, G. (1998) *Introducing Cultural Studies*, Hemel Hempstead: Harvester Wheatsheaf.

Bauman, Z. (1996) 'From Pilgrim to Tourist – or a Short History of Identity', in S. Hall and P. du Gay (eds), *Questions of Cultural Identity*, London: Sage.

Beck, U. (1992) *Risk Society*, London: Sage.

Becker, H. (1963) *Outsiders: Studies in the Sociology of Deviance*, New York: Free Press.

Benamou, M. and Caramello, C. (eds), (1977) *Performance in Postmodern Culture*, Sun Prairie, WI: Baumgartner Publications.

Benjamin, W. (1970), 'The Work of Art in the Age of Mechanical Reproduction', in W. Benjamin, *Illuminations*, London: Jonathan Cape.

Bennett, S. (1997) *Theatre Audiences: A Theory of Production and Reception* (2nd edition), London: Routledge.

Berger, J. (1972) *Ways of Seeing*, London: Penguin/BBC.

Bernstein, C. (1977) 'Performance as News: Notes on an Intermedia Guerrilla Art Group', in M. Benamou and C. Caramello (eds), *Performance in Postmodern Culture*, Madison, WI: Coda Press.

Boal, A. (1979) *Theatre of the Oppressed*, New York: Urizen Press.

Bourdieu, P. (1984) *Distinction: A Social Critique of the Judgement of Taste*, London: Routledge and Kegan Paul.

Bradbrook, M.C. (1962) *The Rise of the Common Player*, Cambridge, MA: Harvard University Press.

Brake, M. (1985) *Comparative Youth Culture: The Sociology of Youth Cultures and Youth Subcultures*, London: Routledge and Kegan Paul.

Brown, M.E. (1994) *Soap Opera and Women's Talk*, London: Sage.

Brunsdon, C. (1990) 'Problems with Quality', *Screen*, 31(1), 67–90.

Bryson, B. (1996) '"Anything but Heavy Metal": Symbolic Exclusion and Musical Dislikes', *American Sociological Review*, 61, 884–99.

Buckingham, D. (1987) *Public Secrets: EastEnders and its Audience*, London: British Film Institute.

Burns, E. (1972) 'Conventions of Performance', in E. Burns and T. Burns (eds), *Sociology of Literature and Drama*, Harmondsworth: Penguin, 1973.

Campbell, C. (1987) *The Romantic Ethic and the Spirit of Modern Consumerism*, London: Routledge.

Carlson, M. (1996) *Performance*, London: Routledge.

de Certeau, M. (1984) *The Practice of Everyday Life*, Berkeley: University of California Press.

Chaney, D. (1993) *Fictions of Collective Life*, London: Routledge.

Clark, T.J. (1984) *The Painting of Modern Life*, London: Thames and Hudson.

Clarke, G. (1990) 'Defending Ski-Jumpers: A Critique of Theories of Youth Subcultures', in S. Frith and A. Goodwin (eds), *On Record: Rock, Pop, and the Written Word*, London: Routledge.

Clegg, S. (1989) *Frameworks of Power*, London: Sage.

Cobley, P. (1994) 'Throwing out the Baby: Populism and Active Audience Theory', *Media Culture and Society*, 16(4).

Cohen, A.P. (1985) *The Symbolic Construction of Community*, Chichester: Ellis Horwood.

Crafts, S.D., Cavicchi, D. and Keil, C. and the Music in Daily Life Project (1993) *My Music*, Hanover, NH: Wesleyan University Press/University Press of New England.

Craik, J. (1994) *The Face of Fashion*, London: Routledge.

Critcher, C. (1979) 'Football Since the War', in J. Clarke, C. Critcher and

R. Johnson (eds), *Working Class Culture: Studies in History and Theory,* London: Hutchinson.

Crow, G. and Allan, G. (1994) *Community Life: An Introduction to Local Social Relations,* Hemel Hempstead: Harvester Wheatsheaf.

Curran, J. (1990) 'Mass Media and Democracy: A Reappraisal', in J. Curran and M. Gurevitch (eds), *Mass Media and Society,* London: Edward Arnold.

Debord, G. (1994) *The Society of the Spectacle,* New York: Zone Books.

Drotner, K., (1994) 'Ethnographic Enigmas: "The Everyday" in Recent Media Studies', *Cultural Studies,* 8(2), 341–57.

Duvignaud, J. (1965) 'The Theatre in Society: Society in the Theatre', in E. Burns and T. Burns (eds), *Sociology of Literature and Drama,* Harmondsworth: Penguin, 1973.

Dyer, R. (1979) *Stars,* London: British Film Institute.

Dyer, R. (1991) 'Charisma', in C. Gledhill (ed.) *Stardom: Industry of Desire,* London: Routledge.

Dyer, S. and Jary, D. (1973) 'Football: A Sociological Eulogy', in M. Smith, S. Parker and C. Smith (eds), *Leisure and Society in Britain,* London: Allen Lane.

Ehrenreich, B., Hess, E., Jacobs, G. (1992) 'Beatlemania: Girls Just Want to Have Fun', in L. Lewis (ed.), *The Adoring Audience: Fan Culture and Popular Media,* London: Routledge.

Eisenberg, E. (1988) *The Recording Angel,* London: Pan Books.

Elliott, P. (1974) 'Uses and Gratifications Research: A Critique and a Sociological Alternative', in J.G. Blumler and E. Katz (eds), *The Uses of Mass Communications,* London: Sage.

Erickson, B. (1996) 'Culture, Class, and Connections', *American Journal of Sociology,* 102(1), 217–51.

Evans, W. (1990) 'The Interpretive Turn in Media Research', *Critical Studies in Mass Communication,* 7(2).

Ewen, S. (1988) *All Consuming Images,* New York: Basic Books.

Featherstone, M. (1991) *Consumer Culture and Postmodernism,* London: Sage.

Fine, G.A. (1983) *Shared Fantasy: Role-Playing Games as Social Worlds,* Chicago: University of Chicago Press.

Fine, G.A. and Kleinman, S. (1979) 'Rethinking Subculture: An Interactionist Analysis', *American Journal of Sociology,* 85(1), 1–20.

Finnegan, R. (1989) *The Hidden Musicians: Music-making in an English Town,* Cambridge: Cambridge University Press.

Fiske, J. (1987) *Television Culture,* London: Methuen.

Fiske, J. (1989a) 'Moments of Television: Neither the Text Nor the Audience', in E. Seiter, H. Borchers, G. Kreutzner and E.-M. Warth (eds), *Remote Control,* London: Routledge.

Fiske, J. (1989b) *Reading the Popular,* London: Unwin Hyman.

Fiske, J. (1992) 'The Cultural Economy of Fandom', in L. Lewis (ed.), *The Adoring Audience: Fan Culture and Popular Media,* London: Routledge.

Flitterman-Lewis, S. (1992), 'Psychoanalysis, Film, and Television', in R. Allen (ed.), *Channels of Discourse, Reassembled* (2nd edition), London: Routledge.

Frith, S. (1983) 'The Pleasures of the Hearth', in *Formations of Pleasure,* London: Routledge and Kegan Paul, 101–23.

Frith, S. (1992) 'From the Beatles to Bros: Twenty-Five Years of British Pop', in N. Abercrombie and A. Warde (eds), *Social Change in Contemporary Britain*, Cambridge: Polity.

Frith, S. (1996) 'Music and Identity', in S. Hall and P. du Gay (eds), *Questions of Cultural Identity*, London: Sage.

Fukuyama, F. (1995) *Trust: The Social Virtues and the Creation of Prosperity*, London: Hamish Hamilton.

Garratt, S. (1984) 'All of Us Love All of You', in S. Steward and S. Garratt (eds), *Signed, Sealed and Delivered: True Life Stories of Women in Pop*, London: Pluto.

Garratt, S. (1994) 'All of Me Loves All of You', in J. Aizlewood (ed.), *Love is the Drug*, London: Penguin.

Gershuny, J. and Jones, S. (1987) 'The Changing Work/Leisure Balance in Britain, 1961–1984', in J. Horne, D. Jary and A. Tomlinson (eds), *Sports, Leisure and Social Relations*, London: Routledge.

Giddens, A. (1990) *The Consequences of Modernity*, Cambridge: Polity.

Giddens, A. (1991) *Modernity and Self-Identity*, Cambridge: Polity.

Giddens, A. (1992) *The Transformation of Intimacy*, Cambridge: Polity.

Gillespie, M. (1995) *Television, Ethnicity and Cultural Change*, London: Routledge.

Giner, S. (1976) *Mass Society*, London: Martin Robertson.

Glasgow University Media Group (1980) *More Bad News*, London: Routledge.

Goffman, E. (1969) *The Presentation of Self in Everyday Life*, London: Allen Lane, Penguin Press.

Goffman, E. (1974) *Frame Analysis*, Garden City, NY: Doubleday.

Goodwin, A. (1992) 'Rationalization and Democratization in the New Technologies of Popular Music', in J. Lull (ed.), *Popular Music and Communication* (2nd edition), Newbury Park, CA: Sage.

Goodwin, A. (1993) *Dancing in the Distraction Factory: Music Television and Popular Culture*, London: Routledge.

Gordon, R. (1995) *It Came from Memphis*, London: Secker and Warburg.

Graves, R. (1960) *The Greek Myths*, Vol. 2, London: Penguin.

Green, N. (1990) *The Spectacle of Nature*, Manchester: Manchester University Press.

Gripsrud, J. (1995) *The 'Dynasty' Years: Hollywood Television and Critical Media Studies*, London: Routledge.

Grossberg, L. (1992a) *We Gotta Get Out of This Place*, London: Routledge.

Grossberg, L. (1992b) 'Is there a Fan in the House? The Affective Sensibility of Fandom', in L. Lewis (ed.), *The Adoring Audience: Fan Culture and Popular Media*, London: Routledge.

Grossberg, L. (1996) 'Identity and Cultural Studies – Is That All there Is?', in S. Hall and P. du Gay (eds), *Questions of Cultural Identity*, London: Sage.

Guralnick, P. (1995) *Last Train to Memphis: The Rise of Elvis Presley*, London: Abacus.

Gurvitch, G. (1955) 'The Sociology of the Theatre', in E. Burns and T. Burns (eds), *Sociology of Literature and Drama*, Harmondsworth, Penguin, 1973.

Hadfield, M. (1985) *A History of British Gardening*, Harmondsworth: Penguin.

Hall, S. (1980) 'Encoding/Decoding', in S. Hall, D. Hobson, A. Lowe, A. and P. Willis (eds), *Culture, Media, Language: Working Papers in Cultural Studies, 1972–79*, London: Hutchinson.

Hall, S. (1982) 'The Rediscovery of Ideology: Return of the Repressed in Media Studies', in M. Gurevitch, T. Bennett, J. Curran and J. Woollacott (eds), *Culture, Society and the Media*, London: Methuen.

Hall, S. (1996) 'Introduction: Who Needs "Identity"?', in S. Hall and P. du Gay (eds), *Questions of Cultural Identity*, London: Sage.

Harrington, C. Lee and Bielby, D.D. (1995) *Soap Fans: Pursuing Pleasure and Making Meaning in Everyday Life*, Philadelphia: Temple University Press.

Harvey, D. (1989) *The Condition of Postmodernity*, Oxford: Blackwell.

Heelas, P. (1992) 'The Sacralization of the Self and New Age Capitalism', in N. Abercrombie and A. Warde (eds), *Social Change in Contemporary Britain*, Cambridge: Polity.

Heelas, P. (1994) 'The Limits of Consumption and the Post-modern "Religion" of the New Age', in R. Keat, N. Whiteley and N. Abercrombie (eds), *The Authority of the Consumer*, London: Routledge.

Heelas, P. (1996) *The New Age Movement*, Oxford: Blackwell.

Hermes, J. (1995) *Reading Women's Magazines*, Oxford: Polity.

Hobson, D. (1982) *Crossroads: The Drama of a Soap Opera*, London: Methuen.

Hoggett, P. and Bishop, J. (1986) *Organizing Around Enthusiasms: Mutual Aid in Leisure*, London: Comedia.

Hornby, N. (1992) *Fever Pitch*, London: Gollancz.

Hornby, N. (1994) 'Sparing the Kid', in C. Roberts (ed.), *Idle Worship: How Pop Empowers the Weak, Rewards the Faithful and Succours the Needy*, London: HarperCollins.

Hornby, N. (1995) *High Fidelity*, London: Gollancz.

Horton, D. and Wohl, R. (1956) 'Mass Communication and Para-social Interaction', *Psychiatry*, 19, 215–29.

Hyams, E. (1971) *Capability Brown and Humphry Repton*, London: Dent.

Jameson, F. (1988) 'Cognitive Mapping', in C. Nelson and L. Grossberg (eds), *Marxism and the Interpretation of Culture*, London: Macmillan.

Jameson, F. (1991) *Postmodernism Or the Cultural Logic of Late Capitalism*, London: Verso.

Jenkins, H. (1992a) *Textual Poachers: Television Fans and Participatory Culture*, London: Routledge.

Jenkins, H. (1992b) ' "Strangers No More, We Sing": Filking and the Social Construction of the Science Fiction Fan Community', in L. Lewis (ed.), *The Adoring Audience: Fan Culture and Popular Media*, London: Routledge.

Jenson, J. (1992) 'Fandom as Pathology: The Consequences of Characterization', in L. Lewis (ed.), *The Adoring Audience: Fan Culture and Popular Media*, London: Routledge.

Katz, E., Blumler, J.G. and Gurevitch, M. (1974) 'Utilization of Mass Communication by the Individual', in J.G. Blumler and E. Katz (eds), *The Uses of Mass Communications*, London: Sage.

Kershaw, B. (1994) 'Framing the Audience for Theatre', in R. Keat, N. Whiteley and N. Abercrombie (eds), *The Authority of the Consumer*, London: Routledge.

Kershaw, B. (1996) 'The Politics of Postmodern Performance', in P. Campell (eds), *Analysing Performance: A Critical Reader*, Manchester: Manchester University Press.

King, A. (1995) 'The Premier League and the New Consumption of Football'. Unpublished PhD thesis, University of Salford.

Kopytoff, I. (1986) 'The Cultural Biography of Things: Commoditization as a Process', in A. Appadurai (ed.), *The Social Life of Things*, Cambridge: Cambridge University Press.

Kuhn, T.S. (1970) *The Structure of Scientific Revolutions* (2nd edition), Chicago: University of Chicago Press.

Lasch, C. (1980) *The Culture of Narcissism*, London: Sphere.

Lash, S. (1990) *Sociology of Postmodernism*, London: Routledge.

Lash, S. and Urry, J. (1994) *Economies of Signs and Space*, London: Sage.

Lewis, J. (1991) *The Ideological Octopus*, London: Routledge.

Liebes, T. and Katz, E. (1993) *The Export of Meaning*, Oxford: Oxford University Press.

Livingstone, S. (1990) *Making Sense of Television*, London: Pergamon.

Longhurst, B. (1995) *Popular Music and Society*, Cambridge: Polity.

Longhurst, B. and Savage, M. (1996) 'Social Class, Consumption and the Influence of Bourdieu: Some Critical Issues', in S. Edgell, K. Hetherington and A. Warde (eds), *Consumption Matters: The Production and Experience of Consumption*, Oxford: Blackwell/The Sociological Review.

Machin, D. and Carrithers, M. (1996), 'From "Interpretative Communities" to "Communities of Improvisation"', *Media, Culture and Society*, 18, 343–52.

McLeod, J.M., Kosicki, G.M. and Pan, Z. (1991) 'On Understanding and Misunderstanding Media Effects', in J. Curran and M. Gurevitch (eds), *Mass Media and Society*, London: Edward Arnold.

Macnaghten, P. and Urry, J. (1998), *Contested Natures*, London: Sage.

McQuail, D. (1987) *Mass Communication Theory*, London: Sage.

McQuail, D., Blumler, J.G. and Brown, J.R. (1972) 'The Television Audience: A Revised Perspective', in D. McQuail (ed.), *Sociology of Mass Communications*, Harmondsworth: Penguin.

McQuail, D. (1994) *Mass Communication Theory: An Introduction* (3rd edition), London: Sage.

Maltby, R. and Craven, I. (1995) *Hollywood Cinema*, Oxford: Blackwell.

Mannheim, K. (1952) 'The Problem of Generations', in *Essays on the Sociology of Knowledge*, London: Routledge and Kegan Paul.

Marcus, G. (1991) *Mystery Train: Images of America in Rock 'n' Roll Music*, London: Penguin (1st edition USA 1975).

Marcus, G. (1992) *Dead Elvis: A Chronicle of a Cultural Obsession*, London: Penguin.

Miller, W.D. (1958) 'Lower Class Culture as a Generating Milieu of Gang Delinquency', *Journal of Social Issues*, 14, 5–19.

Moores, S. (1993) *Interpreting Audiences: The Ethnography of Media Consumption*, London: Sage.

Moorhouse, H.F. (1991) *Driving Ambitions: An Analysis of the American Hot Rod Enthusiasm*, Manchester: Manchester University Press.

Morgan, M. and Signorelli, N. (1990) 'Cultivation Analysis: Conceptualization and Methodology', in N. Signorelli and M. Morgan (eds), *Cultivation Analysis: New Directions In Media Effects Research*, London: Sage.

Morley, D. (1980) *The 'Nationwide' Audience*, London: British Film Institute.

Morley, D. (1989) *Family Television: Cultural Power and Domestic Leisure*, London: Comedia.

Morley, D. (1992) *Television Audiences and Cultural Studies*, London: Routledge.

Murdoch, J. (1990) 'A Villa in Arcadia', in S. Pugh (ed.), *Reading Landscape*, Manchester: Manchester University Press.

Murphy, P., Williams, J. and Dunning, E. (1990) *Football on Trial: Spectator Violence and Development in the Football World*, London: Routledge.

Naremore, J. (1988), *Acting in the Cinema*, Berkeley, CA: University of California Press.

Negus, K. (1996) *Popular Music in Theory*, Cambridge: Polity.

de Nora, T. (1995) 'The Musical Composition of Social Reality? Music, Action and Reflexivity', *Sociological Review*, 43(2), 293–315.

O'Connor, J. (1994) 'Banana Republic: Memories of a Suburban Irish Childhood', in C. Roberts (ed.), *Idle Worship: How Pop Empowers the Weak, Rewards the Faithful and Succours the Needy*, London: HarperCollins.

Pacanowsky, M. and Anderson, J.A. (1982) 'Cop Talk and Media Use', *Journal of Broadcasting*, 26(4).

Page, P. (1962) *The Education of a Gardener*, Harmondsworth: Penguin.

Palmer, P. (1986) *The Lively Audience: A Study of Children and the TV Set*, London: Allen and Unwin.

Parkin, F. (1971) *Class Inequality and Political Order: Social Stratification in Capitalist and Communist Societies*, London: MacGibbon and Kee.

Penley, C. (1992) 'Feminism, Psychoanalysis and the Study of Popular Culture', in L. Grossberg, C. Nelson and P. Treichler (eds), *Cultural Studies*, London: Routledge.

Peterson, R.A. and Kern, R.M. (1996) 'Changing Highbrow Taste: From Snob to Omnivore', *American Sociological Review*, 61, 900–7.

Peterson, R.A. and Simkus, A. (1992) 'How Musical Taste Groups Mark Occupational Status Groups', in M. Lamont and M. Fournier (eds), *Cultivating Differences: Symbolic Boundaries and the Making of Inequality*, Chicago: University of Chicago Press.

Philo, G. (1990) *Seeing and Believing: The Influence of Television*, London: Routledge.

Press, A. (1991) *Women Watching Television: Gender, Class and Generation in the American Television Experience*, Philadelphia: University of Pennsylvania Press.

Pugh, S. (1990) *Reading Landscape*, Manchester: Manchester University Press.

Radway, J. (1987) *Reading the Romance: Women, Patriarchy and Popular Literature*, London: Verso.

Roach, J. (1995) 'Culture and Performance in the Circum-Atlantic World', in A. Parker and E.K. Sedgwick (eds), *Performativity and Performance*, London: Routledge.

Roberts, C. (ed.) (1994) *Idle Worship: How Pop Empowers the Weak, Rewards the Faithful and Succours the Needy*, London: HarperCollins.

Rothenberg, J. (1977), 'New Models, New Visions: Some Notes Toward a Poetics of Performance', in M. Benamou and C. Caramello (eds), *Performance in Postmodern Culture*, Sun Prairie, WI: Baumgartner Publications.

Rowbottom, A. (1994) 'Royal Symbolism and Social Integration', Unpublished PhD Thesis, University of Manchester.

Rubin, J. (1970) *Do It!*, New York: Simon and Schuster.

Rudolph, B. (1991) 'The Supermodels',*Time*, 6(37), 16 September.

Scannell, P. and Cardiff, D. (1991) *A Social History of British Broadcasting: Vol. 1. 1922–1939: Serving the Nation*, Oxford: Blackwell.

Schechner, R. (1985) *Between Theatre and Anthropology*, Philadelphia, University of Pennsylvania Press.

Schechner, R. (1988) *Performance Theory*, London: Routledge.

Schechner, R. (1993) *The Future of Ritual*, London: Routledge.

Schulze, L., Barton White, A. and Brown, J.D. (1993) '"A Sacred Monster in Her Prime": Audience Construction of Madonna as Low-Other', in C. Schwichtenberg (ed.), *The Madonna Connection: Representational Politics, Subcultural Identities, and Cultural Theory*, Oxford and Boulder, CO: Westview Press.

Seiter, E., Borchers, H., Kreutzner, G. and Warth, E.-M. (eds) (1989) *Remote Control: Television Audiences and Cultural Power*, London: Routledge.

Sennett, R. (1977) *The Fall of Public Man*, New York: Knopf.

Shank, B. (1994) *Dissonant Identities: The Rock 'n' Roll Scene in Austin, Texas*, Hanover, NH: Wesleyan University Press/University Press of New England.

Shepherd, J. (1991) *Music as Social Text*, Cambridge: Polity.

Shevstova, M. (1989) 'The Sociology of the Theatre. Part Two: Theoretical Achievements', *New Theatre Quarterly*, May, 180–94.

Shevstova, M. (1992), 'Audiences for Filef Theatre Group's *L'Albero delle rose/The Tree of Roses* and *Storie in cantiere/Stories in Construction*', *Australian Drama Studies*, 20, 93–118.

Silverstone, R. (1994) *Television and Everyday Life*, London: Routledge.

Simmel, G. (1898) 'On the Theory of Theatrical Performance', in E. Burns and T. Burns (eds), *Sociology of Literature and Drama*, Harmondsworth: Penguin.

Smith, G. (1995) *Lost in Music: A Pop Odyssey*, London: Picador.

Somers, M. (1994) 'The Narrative Construction of Identity: A Relational and Network Approach', *Theory and Society*, 23(5), 605–50.

Spigel, L. (1992) *Make Room for TV: Television and the Family Ideal in Post-War America*, Chicago: University of Chicago Press.

Stacey, J. (1991), 'Feminine Fascinations: Forms of Identification in Star–Audience Relations', in C. Gledhill (ed.), *Stardom: Industry of Desire*, London: Routledge.

Stacey, J. (1994), *Stargazing: Hollywood Cinema and Female Spectatorship*, London: Routledge.

Stebbins, R. (1992) *Amateurs, Professionals and Serious Leisure*, Montreal: McGill/Queen's University Press.

Straw, W. (1991) 'Systems of Articulation, Logics of Change: Communities and Scenes in Popular Music', *Cultural Studies*, 15(3), 368–88.

Taylor, I. (1989) 'Hillsborough, 15 April 1989: Some Personal Contemplations', *New Left Review*, 177, 89–110.

Taylor, L. and Mullan, B. (1986) *Uninvited Guests*, London: Chatto and Windus.

Thompson, J.B. (1990) *Ideology and Modern Culture*, Cambridge: Polity.

Thompson, J.B. (1995) *The Media and Modernity*, Cambridge: Polity.

Thornton, S. (1995) *Club Cultures: Music, Media and Subcultural Capital*, Cambridge: Polity.

Tudor, A. (1974) *Theories of Film*, London: Secker and Warburg.

Tulloch, J. and Jenkins, H. (1995) *Science Fiction Audiences: Watching 'Doctor Who' and 'Star Trek'*, London: Routledge.

Turner, V. (1982) *From Ritual to Theatre*, New York: PAJ Publications.

Turner, V. (1986) *The Anthropology of Performance*, New York: PAJ Publications.

Urry, J. (1990) *The Tourist Gaze*, London: Sage.

Wagner, H.R. (ed.) (1970), *Alfred Schütz on Phenomenology and Social Relations*, Chicago: University of Chicago Press.

Walser, R. (1993) *Running with the Devil: Power, Gender, and Madness in Heavy Metal Music*, Hanover, NH: Wesleyan University Press/University Press of New England.

Williams, C.J. (1970) *Theatres and Audiences: A Background to Dramatic Texts*, London: Longman.

Williams, R. (1970) *The English Novel from Dickens to Lawrence*, London: Chatto and Windus.

Willis, P. (1990), *Common Culture*, Milton Keynes.

Wise, S. (1990) 'Sexing Elvis', in S. Frith and A. Goodwin (eds), *On Record: Rock, Pop, and the Written Word*, London: Routledge.

Index

trust, 172–4, 175, 178
Tulloch, J., 126, 141
Turner, V., 40, 46, 47

Urry, J., 34, 80–1, 95, 104–5
uses and gratifications approach,
    7–9, 10, 160

value consensus, 10–11
violence, 4

Wagner, H.R., 118
Walser, R., 6

Weber, M., 101
Williams, R., 47, 150
Willis, P., 24–5, 111–12
Wise, S., 127–8
Wohl, R., 106
women
    magazines for, 108–9
    romance readers, 25–7
    as audience for soap operas, 27,
        154
work lives, television
    references in, 112